THE

COURAGE

TO

BEGIN

A universal concept that applies
to everyone, everywhere, and at
every stage of life

By

Abhijit Bhattacharya

direct or indirect losses incurred because of the use of the information contained within this document, including, but not limited to errors, omissions or inaccuracies.

ISBN: 978-93-341-7479-3

Table of Contents

The Courage to Begin

Introduction

We all dream and have somewhere an aspiration that we will live our life as we dream. However, why is it that so many dreams stay confined to our minds, never translating into real-world action?

This "great gap" between aspiration and action isn't about laziness or lack of will. Often, it's about fear, self-doubt, and a host of unseen psychological forces that keep people anchored to their comfort zone, even when they indeed want to change.

Let's explore why the first step is often the hardest and understand the obstacles standing between people and the lives they dream of.

Aspiration is safe. There's comfort in dreaming because, in our minds, everything goes perfectly. The dream job doesn't come with office politics, the fitness journey doesn't involve aching muscles, and the business venture doesn't risk financial instability. In the sanctuary of our minds, we're free to enjoy our aspirations without the real-world complexities. The moment we decide to act the fantasy meets reality.

This safety net of aspiration creates a "low stake" environment where we don't have to face the possibility of failure. As long as the dream stays a dream, there is no risk of disappointment. While this can feel reassuring, it's also a trap that many people fall into, allowing them to feel content with mere ambition without the need to translate it into effort.

One of the most profound reasons people avoid taking the first step is the fear of failure. This fear isn't irrational, trying something new often does come with the risk of failure. Yet, our minds can sometimes amplify this fear, making it seem larger and more threatening than it truly is. The thought of not succeeding—or worse, confirming to oneself that a dream was "unrealistic"—can be paralyzing.

One of the strongest barriers to action is the internal voice of self-doubt. This inner critic tells us that we're not capable, not smart enough, or not skilled enough. It reminds us of past failures or convinces us that others are more qualified. Self-doubt can be incredibly persuasive, especially if it's been internalized over years.

This voice of self-doubt often grows louder when we're on the verge of doing something important. The closer we get to taking action, the more persistent the inner critic becomes, finding every possible reason to discourage us. Combatting self-doubt requires us to become aware of these inner voices and recognize that they're often rooted in insecurity, not truth. Learning to trust oneself, even in the face of uncertainty, is crucial to crossing the gap between aspiration and action.

Many people believe they need to feel motivated or inspired before they can start working toward their dreams. However, relying solely on inspiration can be a trap. Feelings are fleeting; motivation ebbs and flows, and if we wait for a surge of inspiration to get started, we may wait indefinitely.

The gap between aspiration and action is wide, but it isn't insurmountable. Every journey, no matter how ambitious, begins with a single step. The first step may not bring instant results, but it breaks the inertia, turning dreams into something tangible. The process of starting, despite the fear, self-doubt, and discomfort, is empowering. It signifies a commitment to oneself and the courage to move forward, however small the initial step may.

The power of starting lies in its ability to transform. Once the first step is taken, the journey becomes real, and the distance between aspiration and accomplishment begins to shrink. By acknowledging the barriers and deciding to move forward despite them, we pave the way for growth, learning, and ultimately, success. Each action taken, bridges the gap, bringing our dreams closer to reality.

The dangers of not beginning something new can be subtle yet profound, affecting various aspects of our lives, including our personal growth, relationships, and overall fulfilment. When we resist starting something new, we often fall into a cycle of stagnation that can lead to feelings of regret, frustration, and dissatisfaction.

One of the most immediate dangers is the risk of missing out on opportunities for growth. Each new endeavour presents a chance to learn, develop new skills, and broaden our horizons. By not taking that first step, we deny ourselves the chance to expand our knowledge and experience, ultimately limiting our potential. Additionally, the fear of the unknown can paralyze us, leading to an unfulfiled existence. We may convince ourselves that we are content with our current situation, yet deep down, we may yearn for something more meaningful.

This internal conflict can result in a sense of restlessness and dissatisfaction, as we realize that we are not fully engaging with life. Over time, this stagnation can manifest in various ways, such as decreased motivation, lack of enthusiasm, and even depression.

Moreover, not beginning something new can hinder our ability to adapt to change. In a rapidly evolving world, the willingness to embrace new challenges is crucial for survival and success. By resisting change and clinging to the familiar, we risk becoming obsolete, both personally and professionally. This can lead to missed opportunities for advancement, networking, and growth in our careers, leaving us feeling stuck and undervalued.

In relationships, the failure to initiate new experiences can create a sense of monotony. Whether it's trying a new activity with a partner, reaching out to old friends, or making new connections, the willingness to explore can deepen bonds and create lasting memories. Without these experiences, relationships can stagnate, leading to feelings of isolation and disconnection.

The fear of failure often underlies the reluctance to start something new. We may worry about making mistakes, facing criticism, or not measuring up to our expectations or those of others. This fear can be so paralyzing, it prevents us from even trying. Ironically, by not beginning, we guarantee a lack of progress, while embracing the possibility of failure can lead to unexpected successes and valuable lessons.

Additionally, the danger of complacency lurks when we avoid starting something new. We may settle into routines and habits that no longer serve us, convincing ourselves that it's easier to remain in our comfort zones. However, complacency breeds a lack of motivation and ambition, leaving us unfulfiled. This mindset can lead to regrets later in life as we reflect on the opportunities we missed because we were too afraid or unwilling to take that first step. In the grander scheme of life, not beginning something new can limit our ability to innovate and contribute positively to society. New ideas and ventures are often born from the courage to start.

By refraining from pursuing our aspirations, we not only deprive ourselves of personal growth but also deprive the world of our unique contributions and insights. This can create a ripple effect, where our inaction influences others around us, perpetuating a cycle of stagnation in our communities.

In conclusion, the dangers of not beginning something new are multifaceted and can have a lasting impact on our lives. From personal growth and fulfilment to professional development and relationship dynamics, the fear of starting can lead to regret and dissatisfaction. Embracing new experiences not only enriches our lives but also fosters resilience and adaptability, equipping us to navigate the complexities of the world around us.

The courage to begin is not just about taking a leap into the unknown; it's about opening ourselves up to the endless possibilities that await us. By choosing to step forward, we unlock our potential and create a life filled with meaning, connection, and purpose.

This exploration of the "great gap" between aspiration and action sheds light on the universal obstacles that hold people back. Understanding these barriers and learning to overcome them equips us with the courage and clarity needed to start, transforming our aspirations into achievements.

Chapter 1

The Power of Starting

The power of starting is one of the most transformative forces in our lives. When we start something new—whether it's a project, a lifestyle change, a new habit, or the pursuit of a dream—we activate a psychological shift that brings numerous benefits, both motivating and deeply rooted in human psychology.

The most compelling reason why starting holds such power is that it breaks the cycle of inertia, the mental and emotional resistance that keeps us locked in place, and it taps into our natural drive for growth and achievement. This moment of beginning sets off a chain reaction in our minds, igniting motivation, building momentum, and fostering a profound sense of agency.

Psychologists call this phenomenon ***activation energy***, the initial push required to move from a state of inertia to one of action. Just as in physics, where energy is required to overcome a body's rest, so too does our mind require a burst of psychological effort to overcome the initial resistance to change. Activation energy is often the most challenging part of any endeavour, which is why starting is often the hardest step. However, once we overcome this initial hurdle, we set off a cascade of cognitive and emotional benefits that reinforce our ability to keep going.

One of the key psychological reasons behind the power of starting is that it disrupts a cycle of self-doubt and fear. Fear, especially the fear of failure, is one of the most common reasons people hesitate to start new ventures. The prospect of facing unknown challenges or the possibility of not succeeding can feel daunting, even overwhelming. But when we take the first step, no matter how small, we signal to our mind that we are willing to move beyond fear.

This act of courage helps to reframe our mental landscape. By starting, we begin to replace "what if" questions rooted in anxiety and doubt with empowering "what can be" statements. This shift transforms our relationship with fear, turning it from a roadblock into a signpost on our journey.

Starting also provides a sense of progress, however small, which is crucial for maintaining motivation. Progress is a powerful motivator because it provides a sense of accomplishment and forward movement. Psychologically, seeing progress towards a goal triggers a release of dopamine, a chemical in the brain associated with feelings of pleasure and reward. Dopamine not only makes us feel good but also strengthens our resolve to continue. Each small step reinforces the belief that our efforts matter, that we are capable of achieving what we set out to do. When we start, we make the future feel more tangible, which gives us something to hold on to as we continue.

Another compelling reason for the power of starting is that it gives us a sense of control over our lives. Many of us face feelings of helplessness or passivity in our day-to-day routines, which can lead to frustration and dissatisfaction. When we act toward our goal, we actively choose to steer our life in a new direction, breaking free from cycles of stagnation or complacency.

This newfound sense of control helps boost our self-esteem and fosters empowerment. Instead of seeing ourselves as victims of circumstance, we begin to view ourselves as agents capable of shaping our future. This shift in perception is incredibly motivating and builds a foundation of resilience and confidence.

Moreover, starting creates a ripple effect in our minds, known as *the psychology of consistency*. Social psychologist Leon Festinger's theory of cognitive dissonance suggests that when we commit to a particular course of action, we feel compelled to follow through to avoid a conflict between our actions and beliefs. Starting something new, even with a small action, sets up this desire for consistency in our minds. By making that first commitment, we essentially create an internal momentum that pushes us to maintain alignment between our intentions and actions. The further we go, the more our mind seeks to reinforce the commitment we have made, making it easier to continue as we progress.

The act of starting also feeds into our psychological need for self-improvement and growth. As humans, we are naturally inclined to seek new experiences, challenges, and knowledge. Psychologists often refer to this drive as self-actualization, the desire to realize our fullest potential.

When we begin a new venture, we engage this intrinsic motivation, sparking a sense of purpose and fulfilment. This feeling is further amplified as we develop new skills, gain insights, or reach milestones along the way. Each of these experiences affirms that we are growing, evolving, and moving closer to our ideal selves, which fuels our desire to keep pushing forward.

Starting is often the hardest part of any journey, a truth that resonates with nearly everyone who has ever set a goal, big or small. The excitement of envisioning a goal is natural and almost effortless.

Difficulty of beginning in the right time, right place and right mindset stems from a complex mix of psychological, emotional, and practical factors. While we may have big dreams, aspirations, or even a detailed plan, taking that initial step can feel overwhelming and, at times, paralyzing. Most people spend a significant amount of time preparing, planning, and visualizing their goals, yet find themselves stuck at the starting line.

Imagining the rewards of success, seeing oneself transformed and fulfiled—it's all part of the spark that brings a dream to life. However, the moment we prepare to take action, that spark can quickly feel dimmed by the weight of uncertainty, hesitation, and doubt. What looked inspiring and motivating in our minds can feel intimidating and overwhelming once we're on the cusp of actual movement.

One of the primary reasons for this struggle lies in the gap between where we are and where we hope to be. Starting a journey means embracing change and stepping into the unknown, a place where there are no guarantees of success.

The truth is, trying something new does come with the possibility of failing, of facing setbacks, or even of realizing that a dream is harder to attain than we first thought. This realization can create a powerful mental block, making it easier to hold back rather than risk the vulnerability that comes with beginning.

Another reason that starting something feels so challenging is that, in our minds, aspirations are free from flaws. We hold our dreams in a kind of perfection; they are idealized visions where everything goes smoothly, and we are free from any criticism or judgment.

However, taking action means that these dreams will meet the real world, where obstacles and imperfections are inevitable. The "perfect" business idea may encounter competition, the career change may require learning difficult new skills, and the fitness goal may demand more time and effort than initially imagined.

Action introduces reality, and reality doesn't often live up to perfection. As long as we keep a dream safely in our minds, it remains untested and untouched by failure. But once we take a step, the dream becomes real, and the possibility of it not working out becomes equally real.

Starting is hard, but once we push past that resistance, we pave the way for resilience and progress. Every journey begins with that first, often challenging step, and with each subsequent step, the path forward becomes just a little bit clearer.

The memory of past setbacks can also cloud the optimism and prevent us from taking the first step, even if we have a strong desire to try again. This can manifest in self-doubt, where individuals question their abilities and worthiness to pursue their goals. They might wonder, "What if I'm not good enough?" or "What if I make a fool of myself?" Such thoughts can be powerful enough to create an emotional block that keeps them from even starting.

Psychologically, starting something new taps into the concept of *self-efficacy*, or our belief in our own ability to succeed. When we take that first step, no matter how small, we prove to ourselves that we are capable of taking action toward our goals.

This builds confidence and motivation, reinforcing a sense of purpose and autonomy. The act of beginning, then, isn't just about moving closer to a goal; it's about building the mental belief that we *can* make progress, which propels us forward even in the face of future challenges.

Starting something new often requires a significant amount of mental and emotional energy. The initial phase of any journey demands focus, motivation, and resilience, as individuals must overcome various internal and external obstacles. This energy requirement can feel overwhelming, especially for those who are already dealing with stress or responsibilities in other areas of their life.

For instance, someone who wants to go back to school while working a full-time job may feel that they simply don't have the energy to begin. This perception of limited energy can create a sense of fatigue before they even start, making it harder to summon the motivation to take that first step.

Starting also serves as a catalyst for developing resilience. Once we begin, we inevitably encounter challenges, setbacks, or moments of self-doubt. These obstacles, however, become opportunities to build resilience, a critical trait for long-term success. With each challenge we face, we learn valuable lessons and strategies for handling difficulties. This process strengthens our ability to cope with adversity, making us more capable of handling the complexities of future projects. In this way, the act of starting not only pushes us to begin but also equips us with the psychological tools needed to endure and thrive.

Finally, starting fosters a sense of meaning and purpose in our lives. When we initiate a project or embark on a journey, we often do so because it aligns with something we value deeply. Whether it's personal growth, contributing to society, or creating something of significance, the act of beginning connects us with a larger purpose.

This sense of purpose becomes a source of intrinsic motivation, inspiring us to keep going even when the path is difficult. When we know that what we're doing matters, that it holds meaning beyond immediate rewards, we find the courage to persevere. This connection to purpose is one of the most fulfiling aspects of starting, as it gives us a reason to overcome challenges and keep pushing forward.

Understanding that starting is often the hardest part can help individuals develop strategies to overcome these barriers. One approach is to break the goal down into smaller, manageable steps. Rather than focusing on the entire journey, individuals can start with a simple, achievable action. This helps reduce the sense of overwhelm and creates momentum, making it easier to continue. For example, someone who wants to write a book can start by writing a single paragraph each day. This small action can build into a habit, gradually making the goal feel more achievable.

In conclusion, starting is often the hardest part of any journey due to a combination of fear, self-doubt, perfectionism, and the comfort of familiar routines. These psychological and emotional barriers can create a powerful resistance that keeps people from pursuing their dreams and goals.

However, by understanding the nature of these challenges and developing strategies to overcome them, individuals can find the courage to begin. The journey may be filled with obstacles, but each step forward brings new opportunities for growth, learning, and fulfilment. The courage to start is not just about taking the first step; it's about embracing the possibility of transformation and opening oneself up to the endless potential that lies ahead.

In the Bhagavad Gita, the concept of courage to begin is woven deeply into its teachings, especially as they relate to duty, self-realization, and overcoming inner obstacles. Lord Krishna's counsel to Arjuna serves as a timeless guide on finding the courage to take the first step in any journey, especially when fear, doubt, or uncertainty hold us back.

Another powerful theme in the Gita related to courage is the transcendence of mental obstacles like doubt and fear. Krishna explains that the mind is both a friend and an enemy, depending on how it is disciplined. To begin any journey requires mastery over one's mind and thoughts, overcoming the ego and attachments that lead to hesitation and insecurity. In verse 6.5, Krishna advises, "Elevate yourself through the power of your mind, and not degrade yourself, for the mind can be the friend and also the enemy of the self."

This inner strength and control are the foundation of courage, giving us the ability to take the first step without allowing our doubts to hold us back.

In essence, the Gita advocates for a courageous beginning by encouraging faith in a higher purpose, detachment from results, and mastery over the mind. It teaches that courage doesn't mean the absence of fear but rather acting in alignment with one's deeper principles despite fear.

This wisdom can inspire anyone to begin their journey with resilience and determination, knowing that each step taken with purpose contributes to their spiritual and personal growth.

Chapter 2

Why Starting Can Be Strategic

Starting something new can absolutely be considered a strategic move, especially when circumstances align with clear goals, market opportunities, personal growth, or long-term benefits. While starting often carries challenges—risk, uncertainty, and the inevitable learning curve—it can also be a powerful decision when approached with foresight and planning. Recognizing the right moment to embark on a new endeavour requires self-awareness, industry insights, and an understanding of personal or professional goals. Here's an exploration of why starting can be strategic and the circumstances that make beginning a wise choice.

Starting something new doesn't always mean taking a leap without preparation. In fact, approaching a new beginning as a strategic decision allows for intentional growth, calculated risk, and focused action. Instead of impulsively diving into a new venture or project, a strategic start involves planning, resource allocation, and an understanding of potential rewards and challenges. This approach to starting can help mitigate risks, enhance success rates, and provide clarity on how to best achieve intended outcomes.

Strategic starting also sets a positive tone for long-term success. When you lay out a plan, set achievable milestones, and anticipate potential obstacles, you enter your journey prepared. This level of preparation increases your confidence and helps you maintain momentum even in the face of difficulties. Moreover, a strategic start allows you to leverage your strengths and minimize the impact of areas that may need improvement, creating a well-rounded approach to your goals.

Strategic beginnings can also be beneficial for testing ideas, validating goals, or entering new markets. For example, instead of launching a large-scale business immediately, starting with a pilot program, small project, or prototype allows you to evaluate demand, assess performance, and make improvements. This approach reduces the cost and effort of an initial investment while maximizing the learning you gain from real-world feedback. Here are some circumstances in which starting strategically is especially advantageous.

Circumstances When Starting Something New is Wise

When Market Demand Aligns with Your Skills and Passions

One of the most opportune moments to start something new is when there's a clear market demand that aligns with your existing skills and interests. If you identify an area where you can contribute value and it intersects with a need in the market, starting a project or business in that space can be highly rewarding. For example, if you're a talented graphic designer and see an increasing demand for digital content in industries like marketing or e-learning, that's a strong indicator that launching a design service could meet both your skills and market needs.

Starting strategically in response to market demand can also mean entering an emerging field, such as technology, sustainability, or personalized services. An example of this would be entering the field of renewable energy or eco-friendly products if your background is in environmental science or engineering. When the timing and demand are right, a new venture can be fulfiling and profitable, and you'll have a much easier time positioning yourself as a valuable solution provider to your target audience.

When You've Mastered Your Current Area and Seek Growth

If you've reached a point of mastery or deep expertise in your current area, starting something new can be a great way to expand your skillset and pursue growth.

Experts often find themselves feeling stagnated or unchallenged if they've reached the peak of their field and are no longer learning as much as they used to. Beginning a new project, learning a complementary skill, or exploring a new domain can open up fresh challenges and reignite the excitement that initially fuelled your career.

For example, consider a seasoned software developer who has mastered backend development. To grow professionally, they might consider learning frontend development or venturing into project management or team leadership.

This approach keeps them engaged in their work and positions them to bring additional value to their team or clients. Starting something new when you're already highly skilled in one area helps you evolve, adapt, and remain competitive in an ever-changing professional landscape.

When You're Financially and Logistically Prepared

Starting something new often requires time, resources, and capital. If you're financially stable and have planned for the potential costs of a new endeavour, it's a good time to consider beginning.

Financial preparedness means you won't be burdened by the pressure of immediate success and can take a more thoughtful approach. It also enables you to invest in quality resources, whether that's materials, tools, or support systems, which can significantly impact the success of your project.

Logistical preparation is equally important. If you've planned for the time commitment, have the physical space needed, and are confident in your ability to balance this new start with existing responsibilities, then you're more likely to succeed.

Starting strategically means creating a realistic picture of what you need to get started, allocating those resources, and setting yourself up for success before diving in.

When You Notice a Market Gap or Opportunity

Sometimes, the best reason to start something new is the realization of a unique gap or opportunity. A gap in the market, industry, or even in your personal life can be the spark needed to begin. If you identify an area where needs aren't being met—such as a new service, innovative product, or process improvement—starting a project or business to address that gap can be highly fulfiling and lucrative.

Consider the rise of remote work tools. Before the shift to remote work, there were gaps in how teams communicated and collaborated from different locations. Observing this, many companies started developing tools for remote collaboration, such as project management platforms and video conferencing tools. By starting something new in response to a recognized gap, these companies were able to provide solutions that met the needs of a shifting work landscape.

When You're in a Transition Phase

Transitions—such as a job change, relocation, or personal milestone—can create natural opportunities for new beginnings. During transitional periods, we're often more open to change and inclined to evaluate what we truly want. Starting something new during this phase allows you to build momentum in a positive direction and creates a sense of purpose that can help ground you amid the uncertainty of change.

For instance, after finishing university or taking a sabbatical, many people find themselves at a crossroads. This period offer a chance to start fresh, build new habits, or pursue a passion project that aligns with the life stage they're entering. Similarly, career transitions—such as moving from being an employee to a freelancer or starting a side business—often bring clarity about personal and professional goals, making it an ideal time to begin something new.

When You're Passionate but Lack Fulfilment

Passion is a powerful motivator. If you find that your current activities are not fulfiling, starting a new project or hobby can reignite excitement in your life. Lack of fulfilment may indicate a misalignment between what you're doing and what you're genuinely passionate about. Starting something new in this context can mean pursuing a hobby, building a side hustle, or even making a career shift that aligns more closely with what you love.

When passion aligns with purpose, the journey itself feels rewarding, making the effort and commitment worthwhile. A chef passionate about sustainable eating, for example, might start a blog to share recipes focused on local ingredients. Pursuing passion-driven projects not only brings joy but can also lead to unexpected opportunities and personal growth.

When You're Ready to Build Long-Term Assets

If you're thinking about the future and want to create something that will provide lasting value, starting something new strategically can help you achieve that. Long-term assets—such as a business, investment, or even a personal brand—take time to build, but they pay dividends in terms of financial stability, professional reputation, or personal satisfaction. If you're ready to commit to building a legacy or something enduring, starting with a clear vision and a strategic plan can set you on a path toward achieving your goals.

For instance, starting a blog, YouTube channel, or online course might not yield immediate rewards, but over time, these platforms can generate passive income, establish your expertise, and attract a following. By starting now with a long-term focus, you create opportunities for steady growth and stability.

Conclusion

Beginning something new strategically offers numerous benefits, including preparedness, resilience, and alignment with long-term goals. Starting doesn't have to be a leap into the unknown; it can be a calculated step, grounded in clear purpose, preparation, and planning. By recognizing the right circumstances—whether it's a market gap, financial stability, alignment with passions, or a transitional phase—you can approach new endeavours with confidence.

Starting from a strategic standpoint allows you to embrace the unknown with preparation and insight, ultimately making your journey both rewarding and purposeful. By identifying and acting on the right opportunities, you can turn each beginning into a stepping stone toward personal fulfilment and lasting success.

Chapter 3

Starting From The Start

Starting from the beginning often feels like a daunting, yet necessary step when embarking on any journey. Whether we're pursuing a personal passion, launching a new career, or even taking on a new project, we frequently find ourselves at a crossroads, questioning where we should begin and how to invest our energy. Should we focus on our inherent strengths or should we dive into areas that are currently in demand, even if they are outside our comfort zone? While both approaches have their merits, starting from the foundation of our strengths often provides the resilience, motivation, and personal satisfaction that are essential for long-term success. Here's an exploration of why we should consider starting from the beginning, focus on our strengths, and find ways to balance market demand with our unique abilities.

Why Starting from the Beginning is Important

Starting from scratch may seem like a disadvantage, but it is often a crucial phase in building a solid foundation for future success. Beginning from the ground up allows us to truly understand the process, master the basics, and develop a sense of ownership over our work.

When we dive in headfirst without a solid foundation, we risk missing out on key skills, insights, and knowledge that can only be gained through experience and time. Starting from the beginning allows us to build resilience, problem-solving skills, and adaptability, which are invaluable assets in any field.

In any field, the journey itself holds as much value as the destination. Starting small and growing step-by-step gives us the chance to make mistakes, help from them, and apply those lessons going forward. These experiences can provide critical insights into our strengths and weaknesses and allow us to develop a personalized approach that aligns with our skills and values. By not starting from the beginning, we may encounter obstacles that we don't know how to navigate because we've skipped fundamental steps.

Additionally, starting from the beginning helps to foster patience and humility. Success, especially in any long-term endeavour, requires both attributes. Impatience can lead us to take shortcuts, which may compromise the quality of our work or leave us feeling unfulfiled. Humility helps us recognize that growth is a continuous process and that there is always room for improvement. By starting from the beginning, we give ourselves permission to grow, develop, and refine our abilities over time.

The Value of Focusing on Strengths

Our strengths are often deeply aligned with our passions and natural inclinations. When we focus on what we're good at, we tend to experience more enjoyment and satisfaction in our work. This sense of fulfilment fuels motivation, which is vital for staying committed over the long haul. When we leverage our strengths, we're also more likely to produce high-quality results because we're building on a solid foundation of skill and knowledge. This can create a cycle of positive reinforcement, where the more we engage in our strengths, the better we become, and the more enjoyment and satisfaction we derive from our work.

Strengths also provide a starting point for innovation. When we work within areas where we already have some level of competence, we can push the boundaries and explore new approaches without feeling overwhelmed. This doesn't mean we should ignore areas for improvement, rather focus on building a unique skill set that sets us apart. Working on our strengths can be likened to sharpening a tool—we become more effective, efficient, and skilled, which opens up new possibilities for growth and advancement.

Focusing on strengths also enhances our confidence. When we operate from a place of confidence, we're more resilient in the face of challenges. Rather than feeling uncertain or insecure about our capabilities, we know that we have a solid foundation to rely on. This confidence makes it easier to take risks, innovate, and push past obstacles, which are essential components of any successful journey.

The Role of Market Demand

On the other hand, focusing solely on our strengths may not always align with what the market demands. In an increasingly competitive world, it's essential to consider market trends, industry shifts, and consumer needs. Sometimes, market demand requires us to learn new skills or adapt to new areas, especially if we aim to build a sustainable career or business. There's a strong case to be made for paying attention to what's in demand because it increases our chances of creating value that others recognize and are willing to pay for.

However, it's important to approach market demand strategically rather than jumping on every trend. Trying to master every new skill or pursue every high-demand area can be exhausting and may lead to burnout. Instead, consider aligning your strengths with areas of demand that complement your natural abilities. For example, if you have strong communication skills and there is high demand for content creation, you could focus on becoming an expert in that niche rather than venturing into an area that feels unnatural or uninspiring.

Balancing Strengths and Market Demand

The ideal approach often lies in striking a balance between your strengths and what the market needs. Start by assessing your core skills, passions, and unique attributes, then look for ways to apply them within high-demand areas. By aligning your personal strengths with market trends, you create a unique position where you can offer something valuable and fulfiling. This approach ensures that you're not only competent in what you do but also passionate, making the journey enjoyable and sustainable.

It's also worth noting that market demand fluctuates. Skills that are highly sought-after today may become less relevant tomorrow. By focusing on your strengths, you create a foundation that is adaptable to changes in the market. When your core competencies are strong, it becomes easier to learn and adapt to new skills as the market evolves. This adaptability ensures long-term success and keeps you relevant even as trends change.

Building the Right Mindset to Start from Scratch

Finally, starting from scratch requires a growth-oriented mindset. Rather than focusing on immediate success, it's about valuing the learning process and trusting that small, consistent efforts will yield results over time. When you start with your strengths and apply them to an area of demand, you lay the groundwork for long-term success. Embrace the journey as an opportunity to refine your skills, develop resilience, and create something uniquely yours.

A growth mindset fosters resilience, adaptability, and continuous improvement, which are crucial for anyone starting from scratch. It's about acknowledging that growth is gradual and that setbacks are simply part of the journey. Rather than seeing starting from scratch as a disadvantage, view it as an exciting opportunity to build something that aligns with your values, skills, and passions.

Examples of Some Successful Individuals Who Started from Their Strengths:

Many successful individuals and businesses have thrived by focusing on their strengths rather than chasing every demand. Real-life examples illustrate how these barriers play out in practice. For instance, Apple built its reputation on a focus on design and user experience, even when the tech industry prioritized functionality over aesthetics. This focus on its strengths allowed Apple to create a unique niche, eventually making it one of the most valuable companies globally.

Similarly, **J.K. Rowling** focused on her love of storytelling and literature, rather than pursuing genres or topics in high demand at the time. Her dedication to her craft, rather than trying to write "what sells," allowed her to create a work of art that resonated deeply with readers around the world. By focusing on her strengths, she achieved success that exceeded her wildest dreams.

Similarly, entrepreneurs like **Steve Jobs and Elon Musk** faced significant challenges and failures in their early careers. Both had to overcome immense self-doubt, criticism, and financial obstacles, yet their willingness to start and keep going eventually led them to revolutionize the entire industry.

These examples highlight the courage it takes to start something new, especially when the vision is unconventional or ahead of its time. Each of these entrepreneurs faced uncertainty, criticism, and challenges, but their willingness to take that first step—and to keep pushing forward—was instrumental in turning their ideas into successful enterprises. Their stories remind us that courage and persistence are key ingredients for success in any entrepreneurial journey.

Chapter 4

Overcoming Fear of Failure

Fear of failure is one of the most potent forces keeping us from pursuing our dreams. It's often not the task itself that feels impossible, but the fear that we might fall short. This fear can make the act of starting to daunting us before we even begin.

When we fear failure, we fear more than just not achieving our goals; we fear judgment, rejection, that confirms of our worst insecurities. Failure can seem like a confirmation of our inadequacies, so instead, we play it safe, opting for the comfort of inaction. But in reality, failure is often a natural, even necessary, part of growth. It's through our missteps and mistakes that we refine our approaches, deepen our testament, and build resilience.

Fear of failure may keep us safe from embarrassment or disappointment, but it also robs us of the chance to reach our full potential. Avoiding risk keeps us in the comfort zone, which may feel safe but is ultimately limiting.

Staying in this zone might protect us from immediate disappointment, but it leads to long-term regret, stifling personal growth and the possibility of experiencing the full richness of life's opportunities. Recognizing this trap and transforming our perspective on failure is key to breaking free from its grip.

Reframing Failure as a Learning Opportunity

One of the most effective ways to overcome the fear of failure is by reframing it. Instead of viewing failure as a dead-end or a mark of inadequacy, we can begin to see it as a vital part of the journey. Here are some strategies to reframe failure:

1. View Failure as Feedback:

Every failure is a chance to learn something new. By treating each setback as valuable feedback rather than a personal flaw, we can learn to use it constructively. Each failure tells us something about what didn't work and provides insights for improvement. The more we learn from our mistakes, the better we get at adapting and evolving, which brings us closer to our goals.

2. Separate Failure from Identity:

Often, we take failure personally, seeing it as a reflection of our self-worth. But failure is an event, not a trait. Just because a project or plan didn't work out doesn't mean we're incapable or destined to fail. When we separate our sense of self from the outcomes of our actions, we gain the freedom to try without the weight of self-judgment. Recognizing that failure doesn't define us helps us remain resilient and open to new attempts.

3. Set Small, Manageable Goals:

Breaking down big goals into smaller, achievable steps makes it easier to try without the pressure of immediate success or fear of failure. Small successes build confidence and momentum, while small setbacks are more manageable and less intimidating. This gradual approach also helps desensitize us to the fear of failure, showing us that missteps are part of the process rather than something to avoid.

4.Adopt a Growth Mindset:

With a growth mindset, we see our abilities and intelligence as qualities that can be developed. Rather than fearing failure, we see it as a necessary step toward improvement. This mindset encourages us to embrace challenges and view failures as opportunities to grow. Adopting a growth mindset empowers us to take risks without the fear that failure will have lasting negative effects on our potential.

5. Celebrate Effort Over Outcome:

If we celebrate only our achievements, we reinforce the fear of failure because it suggests that success is all that matters. When we celebrate the effort and courage it took to try, we acknowledge our resilience, creativity, and perseverance. This shift in focus helps us value the journey as much as the destination, building a mindset where trying, even without guaranteed success, becomes an achievement in itself.

Acceptable Limits of Failure

The question of an "acceptable limit" for failure is one that varies depending on the individual, the context, and the stakes involved. In professional settings, personal goals, creative pursuits, and business ventures, failure is not only inevitable but also a critical part of the growth process. We tend to fear failure, viewing it as a sign of inadequacy or weakness, yet the reality is that failures—when approached accurately—provide invaluable insights that propel us toward eventual success. Accepting failure as part of the journey, rather than an obstacle to be avoided, opens up new avenues for resilience, self-discovery, and innovation.

So, is there an acceptable limit to failure? Understanding the role that failure plays and learning how to navigate it without allowing it to demotivate or derail you, is essential for anyone embarking on a personal or professional journey. Here's a deeper exploration into why failure is integral to progress, what constitutes a "healthy" amount of failure, and how to know when it's time to re-evaluate your approach.

The Paradox of Failure: Why It's Essential for Success

The concept of acceptable failure is a paradox because, without failure, it's nearly impossible to achieve true success. If we succeed without struggle, it often means we haven't pushed our boundaries or challenged ourselves enough. Failure signals effort, experimentation, and bravery—the qualities that drive real growth. Thomas Edison famously failed thousands of times before inventing the lightbulb, and when asked about these failures, he said, "I have not failed. I've just found 10,000 ways that won't work." Edison's persistence is an example of reframing failure as learning, rather than something inherently negative.

Failure helps us build a stronger foundation by highlighting areas for improvement, sharpening our focus, and teaching us valuable lessons that only come through experience. By accepting failure, we learn to pivot, adapt, and refine our approach, which ultimately leads us closer to achieving our goals. The "acceptable" limit of failure, then, isn't so much about setting a cap but about understanding when failure serves its purpose and when it might be time to change course.

Factors that Influence the Acceptable Limit of Failure

1. The Nature of the Goal

The type of goal you're working towards has a significant influence on how much failure can be tolerated. High-risk industries, like technology and entrepreneurship, often come with high failure rates. In these fields, trial and error is expected as part of the innovation process, and an acceptable limit for failure may be quite high. Startups, for example, are frequently encouraged to "fail fast and fail often" because every failure brings them closer to a viable solution. By contrast, goals that have immediate and high-stakes consequences, such as medical practices or financial investments, may have a much lower tolerance for failure, requiring stringent planning and preparation to minimize risks.

2. Personal Resilience and Mindset

Each person has a different tolerance for failure, depending on their mindset and resilience levels. Some people can bounce back quickly from setbacks, viewing each failure as a temporary hurdle, while others may find even small failures emotionally taxing.

An individual's resilience is often shaped by past experiences, mindset, and support systems. Those with a growth mindset—the belief that abilities and intelligence can be developed—tend to handle failure better because they see it as an opportunity to improve. Knowing your personal limits for handling failure can help you determine how much you're willing to risk before needing to adjust your approach.

3. The Potential for Learning and Growth

If a failure provides significant learning and insight, it may be worth persisting through multiple setbacks. In fact, one of the most crucial questions to ask after a failure is, "What did I learn from this?" Failures that offer insight into skill gaps, highlight areas for improvement, or reveal unexpected challenges are often acceptable because they bring you closer to your goal. Learning-focused failures are not wasted; they serve a purpose by enhancing your capabilities and refining your approach. When failure leads to learning, there's usually no limit on how often it's acceptable, as long as you continue to evolve and adapt.

4. Available Resources (Time, Money, Energy)

Resources play a big role in determining how many setbacks you can afford. If you have ample resources, you may be able to overcome more failures because you can recover from them financially and emotionally. On the other hand, if resources are limited, you may need to set stricter limits on acceptable failure to ensure you can still pivot without depleting what you need to keep going. For example, a startup might have enough funds to sustain multiple product iterations, while an individual with limited finances might have to reconsider their strategy after just one or two setbacks.

Knowing When to Persevere and When to Pivot

One of the most challenging aspects of accepting failure is recognizing when it's time to push forward versus when to take a step back. This balancing act requires honest reflection, a willingness to adapt, and often, external feedback. Here are some indicators for both scenarios:

When to Persevere

1. You're Making Progress: Even small wins can signal that you're moving in the right direction. If your failures are becoming less significant, or you're seeing improvement in skills, knowledge, or outcomes, it's often worth continuing.

2. You're Gaining Insight: If each failure brings new information that helps refine your approach, it can indicate you're on the right path. Failing while learning is an essential part of the growth process.

3. Passion and Purpose Remain: When the reason you began still drives you, and you have a clear sense of purpose, it's often worth persevering. Motivation and passion can fuel resilience, helping you overcome obstacles that might otherwise deter you.

When to Pivot or Pause

1. Repeated, Unproductive Failures

If you're facing the same failures repeatedly without gaining new insights or progress, it might be time to re-evaluate your approach.

2. Diminishing Returns on Effort

If each attempt is costing more than the previous one, whether in time, energy, or resources, and you're not seeing equivalent gains, this could signal that you need a new strategy.

3. Loss of Purpose or Interest

If your passion for the goal has faded or you're no longer sure why you're pursuing it, it's important to reassess. A lack of motivation can lead to burnout, making every setback feel heavier than it is.

Strategies for Managing and Embracing Failure

How to create a healthy relationship with failure, consider implementing these strategies:

1. Set Realistic Expectations

Avoid placing an all-or-nothing approach on your goals. Recognize that failure is part of the journey and set smaller, attainable goals to maintain momentum and confidence.

2. Learn from Each Setback

After every failure, take time to reflect on what went wrong, what went right, and what you could improve. This approach shifts your focus from the outcome to the process, emphasizing learning over success.

3. Surround Yourself with Support

Having a supportive network can make it easier to cope with failure. Friends, mentors, and peers can offer perspective, encouragement, and practical advice.

4. Celebrate Small Wins

Reward yourself for small achievements along the way. Recognizing progress, even when it's incremental, can keep you motivated and make setbacks feel less daunting.

5. Cultivate Resilience

Resilience is a skill that can be developed over time. Practicing self-care, maintaining a positive outlook, and building mental strength are all ways to become more resilient in the face of failure.

The Importance of Setting Realistic Expectations

Setting realistic expectations is a critical element of achieving success and finding fulfilment in any endeavour, whether personal, professional, or creative. When our expectations are grounded in reality, they help us remain focused, resilient, and motivated even when challenges arise. However, in a world where we're often bombarded with messages of instant success, setting realistic expectations can be challenging. Without careful consideration, high expectations can set us up for disappointment, while low expectations can limit our growth and potential.

Realistic expectations bridge the gap between ambition and capability. When we set our sights on goals that are both ambitious and achievable, we lay the groundwork for continuous progress and lasting success. Setting realistic expectations enables us to manage our time, energy, and resources more effectively, helping us stay resilient in the face of setbacks.

When our expectations are too high, we risk burnout, frustration, and a sense of failure if we fall short. On the other hand, if they're too low, we might lack the motivation needed to push ourselves and achieve meaningful results. Realistic expectations strike a balance that allows us to grow within our capacity and reach new levels of accomplishment over time.

Here are some practical strategies for setting realistic expectations in life and work, along with guidance on how to maintain motivation and resilience while pursuing your goals.

1. Start with Self-Assessment

Before setting expectations, it's essential to have a clear understanding of your strengths, limitations, skills, and resources. Take time to reflect on what you bring to the table, as well as any areas where you may need additional support or development. For example, if you're pursuing a new career, assess your current skill level and experience. Are there knowledge gaps that you need to fill? Are there resources or support networks that could assist you along the way?

Self-assessment helps you develop a realistic picture of where you are right now and what's needed to move forward. This exercise isn't about limiting yourself or underestimating your potential; it's about ensuring that you set expectations that are aligned with your current reality. By recognizing where you stand, you can set goals that are challenging yet achievable, allowing for steady and sustainable growth.

2. Define Clear and Specific Goals

A key element of setting realistic expectations is defining clear, specific goals. Vague or overly broad goals can make it difficult to measure progress and determine when you've reached a milestone. Instead, break down your larger aspirations into smaller, specific objectives. For example, if you want to write a book, set clear expectations for each stage of the process, such as outlining, drafting, revising, and publishing.

SMART goals—those that are Specific, Measurable, Achievable, Relevant, and Time-bound—provide a useful framework for setting clear expectations. Instead of saying, "I want to be healthier," a SMART goal might be, "I will walk for 30 minutes five times a week for the next three months." This goal is specific, measurable, and achievable, and it has a clear timeline. By setting clear goals, you create a roadmap that allows you to make steady progress toward your aspirations.

3. Acknowledge Potential Challenges and Limitations

Realistic expectations account for potential obstacles along the way. While optimism is a valuable asset, it's important to balance it with a realistic understanding of the challenges you may encounter. Consider the potential roadblocks, time constraints, financial limitations, and other factors that may affect your progress. By acknowledging these challenges upfront, you can develop strategies for overcoming them and adjust your expectations as needed.

If you're pursuing a career change while working full-time, recognize that your progress may be slower due to limited time. Rather than expecting to make a complete transition in a few months, set a more flexible timeline that accounts for your current commitments. This approach prevents frustration and allows you to maintain a positive outlook, even when things don't go as planned.

4. Focus on Process Over Outcome

Setting realistic expectations means prioritizing the journey over the destination. When we focus too heavily on the outcome, we may overlook the progress we're making along the way. Process-oriented expectations encourage us to embrace each step of the journey, rather than fixating solely on the end goal.

For example, if you're learning a new language, set expectations around consistent practice rather than fluency within a specific timeframe. By focusing on the process—such as dedicating 30 minutes each day to language study—you create an environment that encourages progress without unnecessary pressure. This approach can reduce stress, making it easier to enjoy the journey and recognize the value of each small accomplishment.

5. Build Flexibility into Your Expectations

Realistic expectations are flexible and adaptable. As you pursue your goals, you may encounter unexpected challenges, changes in priorities, or new opportunities that alter your course. Rather than holding rigidly to your original expectations, allow ~~for~~ flexibility and adaptability. This approach acknowledges that life is dynamic, and adjustments may be necessary to stay aligned with your goals and values.

If your goal is to complete a degree within a certain timeframe, but you encounter a personal or family challenge, flexibility may allow you to adjust your schedule without abandoning your goal altogether. By embracing flexibility, you create space to adapt to changing circumstances while staying committed to your larger vision.

6. Seek Feedback and Adjust as Needed

Feedback is invaluable for refining our expectations and ensuring they remain realistic. Whether it's feedback from mentors, colleagues, friends, or family members, an outside perspective can provide insights that may be difficult to see on our own. Constructive feedback helps us identify areas for improvement and provides reassurance when we're on the right track.

If you're working on a project, seek feedback at regular intervals and be open to adjusting your expectations based on what you learn. For instance, if you're launching a new business, market feedback can help you refine your product or service, leading to more realistic expectations about growth and profitability.

7. Practice Self-Compassion

Self-compassion plays a vital role in setting and maintaining realistic expectations. When we're overly self-critical, we may set unreasonably high expectations, pushing ourselves to achieve perfection and setting ourselves up for disappointment. Self-compassion allows us to approach our goals with kindness and understanding, recognizing that setbacks and mistakes are natural parts of the journey.

By treating yourself with compassion, you create a supportive internal environment that fosters resilience and motivation. Instead of seeing mistakes as failures, view them as opportunities for growth. Self-compassion helps you bounce back from setbacks, stay committed to your goals, and maintain a balanced perspective on your expectations.

8. Continuously Re-evaluate and Adjust Expectations

Realistic expectations are not set in stone. As you grow, learn, and progress, it's essential to revisit and adjust your expectations based on new insights and experiences. Periodic re-evaluation ensures that your expectations remain aligned with your current abilities, priorities, and resources.

For instance, if you've set a goal to run a marathon within a year, but realize that you need more time to train safely, re-evaluate your timeline and adjust it as needed. This approach prevents frustration and discouragement, allowing you to pursue your goal in a way that aligns with your well-being.

9. Embrace a Growth Mindset

Finally, cultivating a growth mindset is fundamental to setting realistic expectations. A growth mindset believes that skills, abilities, and intelligence can be developed through effort, practice, and persistence.

With a growth mindset, you approach your goals with a focus on learning and improvement, rather than being fixated on a specific outcome.

When you embrace a growth mindset, you're more likely to set realistic expectations because you view each step as an opportunity to learn and grow. Setbacks become stepping stones, and progress becomes a measure of growth rather than a final destination. This mindset creates a positive, sustainable approach to achieving your goals and encourages continuous self-improvement.

Setting realistic expectations is a dynamic process that requires self-awareness, flexibility, and a focus on growth. By starting with a clear assessment of your strengths, breaking down your goals, and embracing a process-oriented approach, you can create expectations that empower you to make steady progress. When setbacks arise, remember that they are natural parts of the journey, offering valuable lessons and insights. With realistic expectations, you can approach your goals with resilience, enjoy the journey, and celebrate each step of your success.

Conclusion

While there may not be a specific number of failures one should overcome, the key lies in how those failures are approached. The acceptable limit for failure is determined by the amount of growth and learning each setback brings, your personal resilience, and the resources available to you. By viewing failure as an essential part of the process rather than a final verdict, you can turn each setback into a stepping stone.

Famous People Who Embraced Failure on Their Path to Success

The stories of people who found success after numerous failures serve as powerful reminders that setbacks are often stepping stones to great achievements. Some of the most successful figures in history achieved their goals only after enduring countless failures and rejections.

1. Thomas Edison

Edison is often quoted for his resilient approach to failure. When asked about the many failed attempts he made before inventing the lightbulb, he famously replied, "I have not failed. I've just found 10,000 ways that won't work." Edison's attitude toward failure demonstrates a relentless belief in persistence and innovation. His mindset allowed him to see each attempt not as a failure but as a step closer to success, and this perseverance ultimately led to his revolutionary inventions.

2. J.K. Rowling

Before the global success with the *Harry Potter* series, Rowling faced numerous hardships, including financial struggles, rejections from multiple publishers, and personal losses. Yet, she continued to pursue her dream of becoming an author, even when the odds seemed insurmountable. Her persistence paid off, and her story reminds us that setbacks and rejections are often part of the journey to achieving our dreams.

3. **Walt Disney**

Disney, a visionary in entertainment, faced multiple failures early in his career. He was fired from a news agency for "lacking creativity" and experienced bankruptcy with his first animation company. Despite these setbacks, Disney continued to believe in his vision, eventually creating an entertainment empire. His story shows that believing in one's vision, even when others doubt it, is crucial to overcoming fear and moving forward.

4. **Steve Jobs**

Jobs was famously ousted from the company he co-founded, Apple, after a series of disagreements with the board. This public setback could have defined his career, but instead, he saw it as an opportunity for growth. Jobs went on to create new ventures, including Pixar, which redefined animation. Eventually, he returned to Apple and led it to unprecedented success. Jobs' journey illustrates that failure can be a powerful catalyst for reinvention and can lead to achievements beyond initial expectations.

5. **Elon Musk – Tesla and SpaceX**

Elon Musk's ventures are prime examples of entrepreneurial courage against fear of failure. In the early 2000s, Musk invested much of his personal fortune into Tesla and SpaceX, both highly ambitious and risky ventures. Tesla faced significant skepticism, as electric cars were seen as unfeasible, while SpaceX aimed to disrupt the space industry, which was previously dominated by government agencies. Musk's determination and willingness to take enormous personal and financial risks helped him pioneer the electric vehicle industry and advance private space exploration.

6. **Oprah Winfrey**

Oprah, one of the most influential media personalities today, faced numerous challenges in her early life and career. She was demoted from her first television job and faced significant personal obstacles. However, she used these challenges to fuel her determination, eventually building a media empire. Oprah's story highlights that resilience and self-belief are often more important than avoiding failure.

7. **Colonel Sanders**:

The founder of KFC, Colonel Harland Sanders, faced rejection over a thousand times before finding someone willing to partner with him on his fried chicken recipe. His story shows that sometimes, it takes hundreds of failures to reach the right opportunity.

These stories remind us that failure is often part of the journey toward success. Each of these individuals reframed failure as a lesson, treating it as a stepping stone rather than a barrier. They demonstrated that success is rarely a straight line and that setbacks, no matter how discouraging, are not the end of the story. Embracing failure as a learning opportunity and reframing it as a part of the growth process opens doors to new possibilities and gives us the courage to keep going, even when the path forward is uncertain.

Chapter 5

Building the Right Mindset

One of the most empowering perspectives we can adopt is a growth mindset, a concept developed by psychologist Carol Dweck. A growth mindset is the belief that our abilities, intelligence, and talents are not set in stone but can be developed with effort, learning, and persistence. This mindset stands in contrast to a fixed mindset, where we view our capabilities as limited and believe that challenges or setbacks are indicators of our limits rather than opportunities for growth. Adopting a growth mindset opens doors to greater resilience, creativity, and fulfilment because we begin to see challenges as opportunities for self-improvement, not as threats to our sense of self-worth.

Belief systems have significant impact on our behaviour and the outcomes we achieve. When we operate from a fixed mindset, we tend to avoid risks, fear failure, and feel limited by our perceived flaws or limitations. This outlook can make challenges feel insurmountable because we believe they're evidence of our "natural limits." In contrast, a growth mindset encourages us to view challenges as essential parts of the journey, not obstacles to be feared. This shift in perspective enables us to persist in the face of difficulties, to seek learning in every setback, and to develop skills we never thought were possible.

Here are some actionable steps to help shift from a fixed to a growth-oriented approach:

Cultivate Self-Belief

Believing in your potential is fundamental to building the right mindset. Self-belief isn't just about feeling confident but about trusting your ability to grow, adapt, and persevere. Develop a habit of visualizing success and remind yourself of past achievements, as it helps reinforce your inner confidence. When you believe in yourself, it's easier to stay motivated and overcome self-doubt. This belief can propel you forward, even when circumstances become challenging, keeping you committed to your goals.

Cultivating self-belief is foundational to achieving any goal, as it shapes how you perceive challenges and influences your resilience in the face of setbacks. When you believe in your ability to succeed, you're more likely to take the necessary steps toward your aspirations, even when the path isn't entirely clear. Self-belief acts as a powerful motivator, encouraging you to take risks, step out of your comfort zone, and embrace learning opportunities. Without it, even the simplest tasks can seem daunting, and doubt can deter you from moving forward.

To cultivate self-belief, start by acknowledging your past achievements, no matter how small, and recognizing the strengths that helped you achieve them. This reflection can serve as a reminder that you are capable and resourceful, even when new challenges arise. Building self-belief also means challenging negative self-talk and replacing it with constructive affirmations. For example, instead of thinking, "I'm not good enough," try reframing it as, "I may not have all the answers now, but I am capable of learning and growing." This shift in mindset helps reinforce a positive self-image and a greater sense of possibility.

Surrounding yourself with supportive individuals who believe in you can also strengthen your self-belief. Mentors, friends, or colleagues who recognize your potential can offer encouragement and remind you of your value when doubt creeps in. Ultimately, cultivating self-belief is a continuous process, one that requires patience and practice. But with consistent effort, you can build a strong foundation of self-assurance that empowers you to face challenges, make bold decisions, and pursue your goals with confidence.

Recognize and Challenge Limiting Beliefs

Awareness is the first step in changing any belief system. Start by noticing the thoughts you have about your capabilities and limitations. Do you tend to think, "I can't do this" or "I'm not naturally good at this"? Challenge these thoughts by asking, "What evidence do I have for this belief?" or "Is this a fact or an assumption?" Replacing limiting beliefs with empowering thoughts—such as, "With effort, I can improve"—can help shift your perspective.

Focus on Effort Over Outcome

Rather than measuring success solely by the results, focus on the effort and dedication you put into your work. Embrace a mindset that values growth, persistence, and learning over immediate outcomes. If you're learning a new skill, remind yourself that progress and persistence are achievements in themselves, even if perfection feels far off.

Seek Constructive Feedback

A fixed mindset can make us fearful of feedback, as we may see it as a reflection of our limitations. However, feedback is one of the most powerful tools for improvement. When we approach feedback as an opportunity to learn rather than criticism, we're able to see areas where we can improve. Start by welcoming feedback in small, manageable doses, and remind yourself that it's a resource for growth rather than a judgment of your abilities.

Reframe Failure as a Learning Experience

People with a growth mindset see failure as a teacher rather than a verdict. Instead of dwelling on mistakes, look for lessons within them. Ask yourself, "What can I learn from this experience?" or "What could I do differently next time?" By viewing failure as part of the learning process, you cultivate resilience and develop the habit of persistence.

Embrace Resilience

Resilience is the ability to bounce back from setbacks and challenges. Building resilience involves seeing failures and difficulties as temporary and as learning opportunities rather than as reasons to quit. Resilient individuals tend to keep a long-term view, understanding that obstacles are a part of any worthwhile journey. Cultivating resilience allows you to stay committed when things get tough, viewing each hurdle as a stepping stone rather than a roadblock.

Adopt a Language of Growth

The words we use shape our perception. Rather than saying, "I'm not good at this," try, "I'm working on improving." Adding "yet" to your statements can be incredibly powerful: "I haven't mastered this skill yet" leaves room for future growth and reinforces the idea that progress is ongoing.

Practice Patience and Consistency

Success often requires time, and achieving meaningful goals usually involves steady, consistent effort. Developing patience helps you stay focused on your journey rather than becoming discouraged by slow progress. Consistency, on the other hand, is the foundation of mastery. By committing to daily or regular actions that align with your purpose, you create momentum and gradually inch closer to your goals. Remember, small, consistent efforts can yield substantial results over time.

Surround Yourself with Growth-Minded People

Our environment and the people around us can have a major impact on our mindset. Seek out relationships with people who value learning and growth, who view setbacks as part of the process, and who encourage you to push beyond your comfort zone. Growth-minded individuals can inspire you to adopt similar perspectives, making it easier to maintain a growth-oriented approach.

Practice Self-Compassion

Shifting to a growth mindset doesn't mean we won't experience doubt or setbacks. Self-compassion allows us to acknowledge our struggles without harsh self-criticism. By being kind to ourselves, we create an internal environment where it's safe to try, fail, and grow. This fosters resilience and a willingness to take risks.

Building a growth mindset takes time and conscious effort, but the rewards are profound. As we develop this mindset, we transform our approach to challenges, setbacks, and self-perception. We begin to see ourselves not as static beings but as dynamic individuals capable of continual growth. In embracing a growth mindset, we empower ourselves to pursue goals with confidence and curiosity, embracing the journey as much as the destination.

Chapter 6

Setting Clear Intentions

Setting clear intentions is foundational to The Courage to Begin. When we set intentions, we are not only defining what we want to achieve, but we are also aligning our internal motivations, beliefs, and desires with our external actions. Intentions are more than goals; they are a commitment to a path, a way of being, and a purpose that goes beyond mere achievement. They give depth to our actions and allow us to approach each step with clarity, focus, and commitment.

Setting clear, actionable goals is essential to making progress in any area of life. Goals provide direction and focus, giving us something tangible to aim for and work toward. Without clear intentions, our efforts can feel scattered, making it harder to stay motivated or to track our progress. Setting a goal is the first step in turning dreams into reality; it shifts our focus from vague wishes or wishful thinking is to concrete steps that move us closer to our aspirations.

The critical difference exists between wishful thinking and intentional planning. Wishful thinking is a passive state where we imagine what we'd like to achieve but don't follow it with a plan or actionable steps. It's like wanting to reach a destination without deciding on a route or preparing for the journey. In contrast, intentional planning involves defining what we want, outlining the steps needed to get there, and actively pursuing those steps with purpose and commitment. Planning with intention brings clarity and makes the goal feel achievable rather than distant or unattainable.

Why Set Intentions?

Intentions provide the "why" behind our "what." They clarify why we want to pursue certain goals and what we hope to gain internally from the journey. This intrinsic motivation becomes especially valuable when facing challenges, as it keeps us connected to a deeper purpose that goes beyond superficial rewards. When we are rooted in intention, even setbacks or obstacles become part of the journey rather than hindrances.

By setting clear intentions, we also reduce decision fatigue and simplify our actions. When we know our intentions, we automatically filter out distractions, time-wasters, or decisions that don't align with our values. This clarity can bring a powerful sense of calm, as we are no longer pulled in multiple directions or second-guessing every choice. Instead, we have a clear framework that guides our thoughts, emotions, and actions, making it easier to start—and stay on—our chosen path.

Steps to Setting Clear Intentions

1. Reflect on Core Values

Intentions come from our innermost values. Start by identifying what is most important to you. Ask questions like, "What do I stand for?" and "What do I want my life to reflect?" Your values may include things like honesty, kindness, growth, learning, or independence. Once you're clear on these, you can set intentions that naturally align with your personal values.

2. Focus on Purpose, Not Just Outcomes

Intentions are often focused on who we want to be rather than what we want to achieve. Reflect on the qualities you want to embody, such as resilience, generosity, courage, or creativity. Consider how these qualities can guide your actions. For instance, if one of your values is resilience, an intention could be, "To face challenges with a growth mindset and view setbacks as learning opportunities."

3. **Visualize the Life Aligned with Your Intentions**

Spend time visualizing what life would look like if you consistently lived by your intentions. Imagine how you would act, the decisions you would make, and the way you would feel. This mental rehearsal strengthens your commitment to your intentions and makes it easier to identify opportunities to practice them in daily life.

4. **Break Down Intentions into Daily Actions**

Intentions can feel abstract unless they are tied to actionable steps. If your intention is to live a life of creativity, commit to practicing creativity every day, whether it's through journaling, drawing, or brainstorming new ideas. When intentions are connected to daily habits, they become part of your routine, reinforcing your commitment and making it easier to stay aligned.

5. **Stay Flexible and Open**

Unlike rigid goals, intentions are adaptable. Life may present unexpected opportunities or challenges, and your intentions should evolve to remain aligned with your current self. Staying open to change helps you cultivate a mindset of growth and adaptability, allowing your intentions to shape-shift in response to your life circumstances.

The Power of Clarity

Clear intentions bring clarity to our lives. They reduce the noise of conflicting desires or superficial goals and create a singular focus on what truly matters. This clarity is empowering; it's like lighting a lamp in a dark room, revealing where we need to go and why. The more precise our intentions, the easier it is to start, as we are free from indecision or fear of the unknown. When we are uncertain about our direction, it's often because our intentions are unclear.

Aligning Intentions with Daily Life

Integrating intentions into daily life requires consistent mindfulness. One way to do this is by setting aside a few minutes each morning to reflect on your intentions. Consider writing them down in a journal or stating them aloud as affirmations. As you go through the day, check in with yourself: "Is this action aligned with my intention?" This simple practice can significantly enhance your focus and make starting new projects, tasks, or habits feel purposeful and fulfiling.

To strengthen the connection between intentions and daily actions, some people find it helpful to create a ritual around intention-setting, such as beginning the week with a quiet meditation or setting aside time to review intentions each month. These rituals reinforce the practice, turning it from a thought into a lifestyle.

Setting Intentions as a Source of Inner Strength

Intentions provide a foundation of inner strength, especially when beginning something challenging. They act as a mental anchor, giving us the courage to face discomfort or fear, as we are not acting out of mere ambition but a deep-seated desire to fulfil a purpose. When we feel overwhelmed, our intentions serve as a reminder that we are on a meaningful path, helping us push through initial difficulties with resilience.

Think of intentions as the North Star, guiding us through the fog of uncertainty. They may not eliminate all challenges, but they offer direction and motivation. When we know that our actions are aligned with our highest values, it becomes easier to find the courage to begin, even if the journey feels intimidating or unclear.

Using Intentions to Navigate Challenges

No path is without obstacles, and this is where intentions become crucial. They help us reframe setbacks as learning opportunities and maintain a growth-oriented mindset. When challenges arise, reflect on your intention and ask, "How can I approach this in a way that aligns with my core values?" This perspective not only reinforces your commitment to the journey but also helps you navigate challenges in a way that feels authentic and constructive.

If your intention is to live a life of integrity, facing a challenging situation with honesty, even if it's uncomfortable, aligns with your deeper purpose. Instead of being paralyzed by the challenge, you are empowered to act in alignment with your principles, building courage along the way.

Reinforcing Intentions through Reflection

Regular reflection helps reinforce intentions. Take time to evaluate how your intentions have influenced your actions and the outcomes you've achieved. Reflecting on this connection strengthens your commitment, deepens your understanding, and increases your motivation to stay true to your path.

A powerful way to deepen this practice is by journaling. Record the moments when you acted in alignment with your intentions and the sense of fulfilment that followed. Over time, these reflections build a strong foundation of self-belief, reminding you of the progress you're making and empowering you to continue forward.

One of the best ways to set effective goals is by using the SMART criteria. SMART goals provide a structured approach to goal setting, making it easier to create a clear, actionable path toward achieving what we desire.

How to use the SMART framework

1. Specific

Goals should be clear and specific, answering the questions of who, what, where, when, and why. Specificity helps us to visualize the outcome and stay focused. Instead of saying, "I want to get fit," a specific goal might be, "I want to lose 10 pounds by exercising four times a week and eating healthier."

2. Measurable

A goal should have criteria that allow you to track your progress. Measurable goals provide benchmarks that help you stay motivated and gauge whether you're moving in the right direction. In the fitness example, tracking weight loss, workout frequency, or even changes in energy levels are measurable elements that show progress.

3. Achievable

Goals should be realistic and attainable given your current resources and limitations. While goals should push you to grow, setting unrealistic ones can lead to discouragement. Assess your current situation and consider what steps will be challenging yet possible. If your goal is to save a certain amount of money, evaluate your income and expenses to set a savings target that you can realistically reach.

4. Relevant

Ensure the goal aligns with your broader values and long-term objectives. If a goal doesn't resonate with your personal values or doesn't contribute to your overall purpose, it can feel empty or unsustainable. Relevant goals create a sense of connection between what you're working on now and where you want to be in the future, making the journey meaningful.

5. Time-Bound

Every goal needs a deadline. A time frame gives you a sense of urgency and a structure for breaking down tasks. Deadlines help prevent procrastination and give you milestones to celebrate as you progress. Instead of "I want to learn a new language," a time-bound version would be, "I want to complete a beginner course in Spanish within three months."

Example of a SMART Goal

Let's apply the SMART framework to a goal of improving career skills:

- **Specific**: "I want to complete an online certification in Artificial Intelligence."

- **Measurable**: "I will track my progress by completing weekly modules and assignments."

- **Achievable**: "The certification course requires five hours per week, which fits into my schedule."

- **Relevant**: "This certification aligns with my goal to advance in my current job role."

- **Time-Bound**: "I will complete the course and earn my certification within one year."

With the SMART framework, this goal becomes clear and manageable, with specific steps and timelines to guide action and track progress.

Setting clear, intentional goals transforms aspirations into actionable plans, helping us achieve meaningful outcomes. By applying the SMART criteria, we can turn dreams into well-defined steps that drive growth and bring our visions closer to reality.

Why Clear Intentions Lead to Courage ?

Clear intentions provide a unique kind of courage, one that is rooted in conviction rather than mere confidence. Knowing why we are doing something gives us a sense of purpose that propels us forward even when fear, doubt, or external pressures arise. This courage is not a fleeting feeling but a deeply ingrained belief that we are on the right path, giving us the strength to start and persist, regardless of obstacles.

Ultimately, setting clear intentions is about more than achieving specific goals; it's about living in alignment with our values and purpose. It's about cultivating a life that reflects who we are at our core and using that as the driving force behind every beginning. With clear intentions, we are no longer just chasing success or external validation; we are pursuing a meaningful path that empowers us, fulfils us, and gives us the courage to begin—again and again.

Chapter 7

Embracing Discomfort

Dealing with discomfort after beginning something important is one of the most challenging yet transformative experiences in any journey. The excitement of starting can quickly give way to doubts, fear, and frustration as we encounter the inevitable hurdles that arise. But it is precisely in these moments of discomfort that real growth occurs. Learning to navigate the uncomfortable periods is essential for building resilience, perseverance, and a deep-seated courage that goes beyond just the thrill of beginning.

Discomfort often appears after the initial momentum fades and the reality of the journey sets in. The newness and excitement can carry us through the first steps, but as challenges arise, we're confronted with aspects of ourselves that resist change. This resistance is natural; it's our mind's way of protecting us from perceived threats or failure. But the very act of pushing through discomfort is what distinguishes those who succeed from those who give up.

Discomfort is a Natural Part of the Process

The first step in dealing with discomfort is to shift how we perceive it. Many people invalidate discomfort as inadequacy. In reality, discomfort is a natural and necessary part of any significant endeavours. Just as a muscle grows stronger through the strain of exercise, our mental and emotional resilience is built through facing challenges. Discomfort signals that we are stepping outside our comfort zones, which is where growth happens.

The discomfort you face after beginning a new journey is a sign that you're pushing beyond what is familiar and easy. It's an indication that you are growing, challenging your limits, and setting the stage for new possibilities. When you embrace discomfort as part of the process, it loses some of its power over you. Rather than seeing it as something to be avoided, you can view it as a signal that you're moving in the right direction.

To steer discomfort effectively, it's important to develop mental resilience. This resilience is often built by accepting that discomfort is unavoidable and choosing to face it rather than resist it. A useful technique is to acknowledge the discomfort without judgment. When you feel stressed, overwhelmed, or doubtful, instead of pushing these feelings away, pause and observe them. Recognize that it's okay to feel uncomfortable and remind yourself that this feeling won't last forever.

Acceptance allows you to move forward without being controlled by your emotions. When you resist discomfort, it often grows stronger because you're focusing on it and trying to make it go away. By accepting it as part of the journey, you can maintain your focus on the tasks at hand, rather than getting lost in feelings of self-doubt or frustration.

Reconnecting with Your "Why"

When the going gets tough, it's essential to remind yourself why you began in the first place. Your "why" is the underlying reason or purpose that motivated you to start this journey. Whether it's a personal goal, a dream, or a commitment to better yourself, reconnecting with your original intention can provide renewed energy and clarity.

Take time to reflect on what this journey means to you and how it aligns with your values. Visualize the outcome you desire and the positive impact it will have on your life. Write down your reasons for beginning and place them somewhere visible, such as on your desk or your phone's home screen. This simple practice can act as a powerful anchor, grounding you when doubts and discomfort try to pull you off course.

Seeking Support and Community

When dealing with discomfort, don't underestimate the power of support from others. Surround yourself with people who understand your journey, whether they're friends, mentors, or others working toward similar goals. Sharing your experiences and challenges with someone who understands can provide comfort and perspective, reminding you that you're not alone.

Community support can be a lifeline during tough times. Hearing others' stories, learning how they've overcome challenges, and receiving encouragement can all help boost your resilience. Additionally, having an accountability partner or joining a group related to your goal can motivate you to keep going, especially when you feel like giving up.

Reframing Discomfort as a Learning Opportunity

Every challenge, every moment of discomfort, holds potential for growth. When we approach discomfort with curiosity rather than circumvention, we open ourselves to valuable lessons. Ask yourself, "What can I learn from this experience?" This question can shift your mindset from one of resistance to one of openness and exploration.

Reframing discomfort as an opportunity to learn also lessens its intensity. When you view challenges as stepping stones rather than obstacles, they become less daunting and more empowering. This shift in perspective can help you develop a growth-oriented mindset, one that sees every challenge as an opportunity to build courage, resilience, and adaptability.

Practicing Mindfulness to Stay Grounded

Mindfulness is a powerful tool for managing discomfort. By staying present in the moment, you can prevent your mind from wandering into worst-case scenarios and self-doubt. Mindfulness allows you to observe your thoughts and emotions without becoming attached to them, helping you maintain a sense of calm even in the face of discomfort.

Practicing mindfulness can be as simple as taking a few deep breaths when you start feeling overwhelmed. Focus on the present task and try not to let your mind dwell on past mistakes or future worries. This practice can help you stay grounded and focused, making it easier to push through tough moments.

Ultimately, dealing with discomfort is about building emotional resilience—the ability to remain calm, focused, and determined in the face of adversity. Each time you push through discomfort, you are building this resilience. Over time, the challenges that once felt overwhelming will seem more manageable, and your confidence in your ability to handle discomfort will grow.

Resilience is like a muscle: the more you work it, the stronger it gets. Each time you face discomfort, remind yourself that you're building your capacity to handle life's ups and downs. This mindset helps you approach future challenges with greater courage and a sense of self-assuredness.

Facing discomfort and learning to deal with it is a cornerstone of developing the courage to begin any journey, goal, or transformation. Discomfort is a natural part of stepping outside our comfort zones, where true growth occurs. When we willingly face discomfort, we train ourselves to navigate unfamiliar situations and gradually build resilience. This resilience is essential for buidling courage because it reduces the fear of failure or hardship, empowering us to take that critical first step, no matter how daunting it may seem.

Embracing discomfort teaches us that challenges and setbacks are temporary and surmountable, reinforcing the belief that we are capable of handling adversity. Each time we confront discomfort, we gain a bit more confidence in our ability to overcome obstacles, making us more willing to begin something new, even if it involves uncertainty or risk. Moreover, dealing with discomfort shifts our perspective, helping us see that discomfort isn't necessarily a sign of failure but a sign of growth in progress.

In a way, discomfort becomes a teacher, guiding us toward self-discovery and fortitude. By making peace with the uneasiness that often accompanies new beginnings, we prepare ourselves to act boldly, recognizing that courage doesn't come from avoiding discomfort but from learning to carry it forward with purpose.

Personal growth and comfort rarely coexist. True growth requires us to step outside of our familiar routines and take on challenges that stretch our skills, mindsets, and resilience. Comfort zones offer safety and predictability but can also hold us back from reaching our full potential. By staying within these boundaries, we avoid discomfort but sacrifice new learning, innovation, and transformation. Embracing discomfort, on the other hand, pushes us to face fears, take risks, and explore possibilities that lead to personal growth.

When we venture into unknown territory, we expose ourselves to failure, judgment, or even rejection—factors that which can be intimidating. But by leaning into these challenges, we find ourselves capable of more than we imagined. Small steps into discomfort accumulate over time, broadening our horizons and building resilience. The initial discomfort fades as we gain experience, turning what was once challenging into a new normal, and making way for further growth.

The discomfort of pursuing challenging goals is part of the journey, and learning to push through those feelings can be incredibly rewarding.

Strategies to help stay motivated when the going gets tough

1. **Visualize Your Long-Term Goals**

Reminding yourself of the end goal can make temporary discomfort feel more worthwhile. Visualize what achieving your goal will feel like, and imagine the benefits it will bring. This mental exercise keeps your focus on the bigger picture, making short-term challenges feel manageable.

2. **Break It Down into Small Steps**

Facing a large, daunting goal all at once can be overwhelming, which is why breaking it down into smaller, more manageable steps is essential. Each small accomplishment builds confidence, helping you to keep moving forward. Progress, no matter how small, reinforces your commitment and reduces the initial discomfort.

3. **Celebrate Small Wins**

Each step forward, however minor, is worth acknowledging. Recognizing small achievements keeps you motivated and makes the larger goal feel more attainable. Celebrating these small victories gives you a sense of momentum, turning challenging tasks into a rewarding journey.

4. Embrace Failure as a Learning Tool

Stepping out of your comfort zone often comes with setbacks. Rather than letting these challenges discourage you, view them as valuable learning opportunities. Every failure reveals areas for improvement and brings insights that make you stronger. By treating mistakes as part of the process, you'll find it easier to face discomfort without the fear of falling short.

5. Practice Self-Compassion

Facing discomfort and setbacks can lead to self-doubt. Practicing self-compassion helps you recognize that growth is challenging for everyone and that you don't need to be perfect to make progress. When you're kind to yourself, you're more likely to continue pushing forward, even when things are tough.

6. Use the "Five-Minute Rule"

If starting a task feels too overwhelming, commit to doing it for just five minutes. Often, the hardest part of challenging work is beginning. After five minutes, you may find it easier to continue. This strategy tricks your brain into taking action without the pressure of immediate perfection or results.

7. Find Purpose in the Discomfort

Remind yourself of why you chose this path and the benefits of enduring short-term discomfort. Purpose provides meaning to challenging moments, transforming them from obstacles into stepping stones toward a greater good. Keep your purpose front and centre as you move forward.

8. **Seek Support from Others**

Surround yourself with people who have been where you are or who are on a similar journey. Whether it's through mentors, friends, or support groups, having people who encourage you can make a huge difference. They can offer guidance, celebrate your wins, and remind you that discomfort is part of growth.

The Reward of Perseverance

While discomfort can be intense, the reward for pushing through is often greater than anticipated. Each time you overcome a tough challenge, you not only patch closer to your goal but also gain a deep sense of accomplishment and pride. This sense of achievement reinforces the courage to begin future endeavours, knowing you have the resilience to handle whatever comes your way.

By embracing discomfort as part of the journey, cultivating resilience, and staying connected to your purpose, you develop the courage to persevere, even when things get tough. This is where true growth lies—not just in beginning, but in continuing through the challenges, emerging stronger, wiser, and more capable than before.

Embracing discomfort is not about seeking struggle but about understanding that growth requires us to confront our limits. When we push through the initial feelings of unease, we expand what we're capable of, transforming what once seemed difficult into a new strength. By seeing discomfort as part of a journey toward something meaningful, we gain the resilience and courage to pursue our highest potential.

Chapter 8

Building Daily Habits

Building daily habits is essential for developing the courage to begin because consistent, small actions build momentum, strengthen discipline, and create a solid foundation for taking on larger challenges. When we cultivate positive habits, we make daily progress toward our goals and overcome internal resistance more easily. This incremental progress boosts our confidence and empowers us to face new, uncertain situations with a greater sense of preparedness and resilience.

Daily habits also help in rewiring our mindset, training us to see tasks as achievable through persistence rather than as hurdles. Habits such as setting clear intentions each morning, engaging in physical exercise, practicing mindfulness, or spending time on personal growth are all small but significant actions that reinforce courage by reinforcing belief in our abilities. Through routine and repetition, these habits nurture a mindset focused on growth and commitment, gradually reducing our fears and doubts.

In essence, daily habits ground us in a rhythm of continuous improvement and self-empowerment. They remind us that courage is not a single act but a practice, built up over time through intentional effort and perseverance. When we master the discipline of daily habits, we prepare ourselves to take on bigger, bolder steps, cultivating the courage to begin new ventures and pursue our aspirations.

Consistent habits are the building blocks of long-term success. While lofty aspirations and grand goals can inspire us, it's the daily actions—often small and seemingly insignificant—that ultimately determine our trajectory. Success is rarely a single monumental event; rather, it's the accumulation of choices made consistently over time. When we cultivate effective habits, we create a foundation that supports our goals and propels us forward, making it easier to stay on track even when motivation wanes.

Discipline and routine play critical roles in habit formation. Discipline helps us push through resistance and distractions, enabling us to prioritize our goals even when we don't feel like it. Routine provides a structure that makes it easier to integrate new habits into our lives. When we establish routines, we create a framework that encourages consistency, turning actions into automatic behaviours over time. The more consistent we are in our routines, the more effortless the habits become, allowing us to channel our energy toward achieving our objectives rather than wrestling with indecision.

Practical strategies for building habits:

1. **Start Small**

Begin with manageable changes that feel attainable. Instead of overhauling your entire lifestyle overnight, focus on one small habit at a time. For example, if your goal is to exercise more, start with just five minutes a day. Once that becomes a routine, gradually increase the duration or intensity. This approach reduces overwhelm and builds confidence, making it easier to adopt more significant changes down the line.

2. **Set Clear Intentions**

Define your habits clearly and specifically. Vague intentions like "I want to read more" can lead to confusion and inconsistency. Instead, say, "I will read for 20 minutes every morning before breakfast." Clear intentions provide structure and make it easier to measure your progress.

3. Use Habit Stacking

Leverage existing habits to create new ones through a technique known as habit stacking. This involves linking a new habit to an already established one. For example, if you want to start meditating, do it right after brushing your teeth each morning. This technique capitalizes on your existing routines, making it easier to incorporate new behaviours.

4. Track Your Progress

Keeping a record of your habits can boost motivation and accountability. Use a habit tracker app, a journal, or a simple calendar to mark each day you successfully complete your desired habit. Visual reminders of your progress can provide a sense of accomplishment and reinforce your commitment to consistency.

5. Make It Enjoyable

Integrating enjoyment into your habits can help you stay motivated. Find ways to make the process fun and rewarding. For instance, if you want to eat healthier, explore new recipes and cooking techniques that excite you. When habits are enjoyable, they become easier to maintain over the long term.

6. Create an Environment that Supports Your Habits

Design your surroundings to facilitate the habits you want to develop. If you want to write more, create a designated writing space that inspires creativity. If you aim to eat healthier, stock your kitchen with nutritious options and remove junk food. By shaping your environment, you minimize friction and increase the likelihood of sticking to your goals.

7. Establish Accountability

Share your goals with friends or family who can support your efforts and hold you accountable. You can also join groups or communities with similar goals. Having others invested in your success creates a network of support that can help you stay committed, especially when motivation falters.

8. Practice Patience and Forgiveness

Building new habits takes time and persistence. It's natural to experience setbacks or slip-ups along the way. When this happens, practice self-compassion and forgive yourself instead of dwelling on perceived failures. Remember that progress is not always linear, and each step—forward or backward—provides valuable lessons.

9. Reflect and Adjust

Regularly evaluate your habits to ensure they align with your evolving goals. Reflect on what's working and what isn't, and be willing to make adjustments as needed. This practice of self-reflection allows you to stay adaptable and responsive to your own needs.

By emphasizing consistent habits and cultivating discipline and routine, we create a powerful framework for long-term success. Each small step taken today contributes to the larger journey, reinforcing our commitment and moving us closer to our aspirations. As we integrate effective habits into our daily lives, we become more resilient and empowered, unlocking our potential for growth and achievement.

Chapter 9

Navigating Doubt and Criticism

Navigating the turbulent waters of self-doubt and criticism is an inevitable part of any personal growth journey. Whether we are pursuing a new goal, launching a project, or seeking to improve ourselves, the voices of doubt—both internal and external—can creep in, challenging our confidence and resolve. While self-doubt can lead to paralyzing fear, criticism from others can feel like an assault on our worth and capabilities. However, learning to handle these challenges constructively is crucial for personal development and long-term success.

Self-doubt often manifests as an internal dialogue filled with uncertainty and negative self-assessment. We may question our abilities, compare ourselves unfavourably to others, or worry that we aren't worthy of our aspirations. This inner critic can be relentless, but it's important to recognize that self-doubt is a common experience shared by many, including highly successful individuals. Understanding that these feelings don't define our potential is the first step in overcoming them.

When it comes to external criticism, it can be particularly challenging. Negative feedback can sting, especially if it feels unwarranted or comes from someone we respect. However, not all criticism is inherently bad. It can offer valuable insights that lead to growth, but it's crucial to differentiate between constructive feedback that can aid our development and destructive criticism that seeks to undermine our confidence.

Strategies for building resilience in the face of doubt and criticism:

1. Acknowledge Your Feelings

The first step in managing self-doubt and criticism is to acknowledge our feelings as and when they arise. Denying or suppressing negative emotions can lead to greater anxiety. Instead, give yourself permission to feel what you feel—whether it's doubt, fear, or frustration. This acknowledgment can provide clarity and serve as a springboard for growth.

2. Seek Constructive Feedback

When faced with criticism, evaluate its source and intention. Constructive feedback is aimed at helping you improve and is delivered with respect and consideration. If feedback feels hurtful or malicious, remind yourself that it often says more about the critic than about you. Seek out those whose opinions you trust, and view their feedback as an opportunity for growth rather than an attack.

3. Reframe Negative Thoughts

Cognitive restructuring is a powerful tool for combating self-doubt. When you notice negative thoughts creeping in, challenge them. Ask yourself whether the thoughts are based on facts or assumptions. Replace self-critical statements with more empowering affirmations. For instance, instead of thinking, "I'll never be good at this," reframe it as, "I am learning and improving every day."

4. Practice Self-Compassion

Treat yourself with the same kindness and understanding you would offer a friend. Recognize that everyone makes mistakes and experiences setbacks. Self-compassion allows you to approach challenges with a sense of warmth and acceptance, reducing the sting of criticism and self-doubt. Engage in positive self-talk and remind yourself of your strengths and past successes.

5. Build a Support System

Surround yourself with positive, encouraging individuals who uplift and inspire you. Seek out mentors, friends, or support groups that understand your journey and can provide perspective during tough times. Having a solid support system can serve as a buffer against self-doubt and criticism, reinforcing your confidence and resilience.

6. Focus on Your Values and Goals

Return to your core values and the reasons behind your pursuits. When faced with doubt or criticism, remind yourself of what truly matters to you and why you started. This reconnection with your purpose can help you maintain perspective and motivation, serving as a guiding light during turbulent times.

7. Practice Persistence

Resilience is built through persistence. Understand that growth is a journey, and setbacks are part of that process. Commit to pushing through the discomfort of doubt and criticism, knowing that persistence will ultimately lead to progress. Each time you face doubt and choose to continue, you strengthen your resilience and deepen your commitment to your goals.

8. Celebrate Your Achievements

Take time to acknowledge and celebrate your successes, no matter how small. This practice reinforces your self-worth and counteracts negative feelings. Creating a habit of self-validation reminds you of your capabilities and helps you stay focused on your progress.

9. Create a Personal Affirmation Practice

Develop a set of personal affirmations that resonate with you and reinforce your worth and capabilities. Repeating these affirmations regularly can help combat self-doubt and create a more positive self-image.

In navigating doubt and criticism, the key is to cultivate resilience through self-validation and persistence. By acknowledging your feelings, reframing negative thoughts, and surrounding yourself with supportive individuals, you can turn self-doubt into a catalyst for growth. Embracing this process with patience and determination will lead you to a more empowered and authentic version of yourself.

Chapter 10

Finding Your Inner Strength

In the journey of personal growth and achievement, obstacles are inevitable. Life has a way of presenting challenges that can test our resolve, shake our confidence, and cause us to question our capabilities. However, within each of us lies an inner strength that can be harnessed to overcome these hurdles and push forward toward our goals. Tapping into this inner reservoir of resilience not only helps us navigate challenges but also fosters a deeper connection to our core purpose—the "why" that drives us.

When faced with obstacles, the first step in finding your inner strength is to recognize that you possess the capability to overcome adversity. Inner strength is often defined by our ability to remain steadfast in the face of difficulties, to draw upon our resources, and to emerge from trials more resilient than before. This strength is not necessarily about being fearless; rather, it is about acknowledging fear and still choosing to take action.

Tapping into Inner Strength

To tap into your inner strength during challenging times, consider the following approaches:

1. **Reflect on Past Resilience**: Think back to times when you faced difficulties and emerged stronger. Reflecting on these experiences can remind you of your ability to overcome challenges. Recall the strategies you employed and the strengths you exhibited. This reflection reinforces your belief in your capacity to handle current and future obstacles.

2. **Practice Mindfulness**: Mindfulness techniques can help you become more aware of your thoughts and emotions. By grounding yourself in the present moment, you can gain clarity and perspective, enabling you to approach challenges with a calmer mindset. Techniques such as deep breathing, meditation, or journaling can enhance your self-awareness and help you tap into your inner resources.

3. **Visualize Success**: Visualization is a powerful tool for accessing inner strength. Spend time imagining

yourself overcoming obstacles and achieving your goals. This practice not only boosts confidence but also creates a mental roadmap for navigating challenges. The more vividly you visualize success, the more likely you are to manifest it in reality.

Staying Focused on Your "Why"

Understanding your core purpose—the "why" behind your aspirations—is essential when challenges arise. This sense of purpose provides motivation and direction, serving as a guiding light during tough times. Here are ways to remain focused on your "why":

1. **Articulate Your Purpose**: Write down your core values, beliefs, and reasons for pursuing your goals. Having a clear articulation of your "why" creates a touchstone you can refer back to when faced with difficulties. This reminder can reignite your passion and commitment.

2. **Connect with Your Emotions**: Your "why" is often tied to deep-seated emotions. Reflect on the feelings associated with your goals—joy, fulfilment, passion, or even a desire to make a difference. Connecting with these emotions can fuel your determination, making it easier to persevere through challenges.

3. **Create a Vision Board**: Visual representations of your goals can keep your "why" front and centre. Create a vision board filled with images, quotes,

and symbols that resonate with your aspirations. Place it somewhere visible to remind yourself of your purpose daily.

Techniques for Mental Fortitude and Endurance

Building mental fortitude is essential for sustaining your efforts and overcoming obstacles. Here are some techniques to develop resilience and endurance:

1. **Set Incremental Goals**: Break down your larger goals into smaller, achievable milestones. This approach not only makes your goals feel more manageable but also allows you to celebrate small victories along the way. Each accomplishment reinforces your mental strength and motivates you to keep going.

2. **Cultivate a Positive Mindset**: Focus on positive affirmations and thoughts that encourage growth and resilience. Surround yourself with positive influences, whether through uplifting quotes, motivational podcasts, or supportive relationships. A positive mindset can empower you to navigate obstacles with confidence.

3. **Practice Gratitude**: Cultivating gratitude helps shift your focus from challenges to the positive aspects of your life. Maintaining a gratitude journal can remind you of what you

appreciate, even in difficult times. This practice fosters resilience by highlighting the good amidst adversity.

4. **Engage in Physical Activities**: Physical activity is not only beneficial for your body but also for your mind. Exercise releases endorphins, which can enhance your mood and alleviate stress. Incorporating regular physical activity into your routine can help you build endurance, both physically and mentally.

5. **Embrace Adaptability**: Developing flexibility in your approach to challenges is key to mental fortitude. Understand that setbacks are a natural part of any journey. Embrace change and view challenges as opportunities for growth rather than insurmountable barriers.

6. **Seek Inspiration**: Draw inspiration from others who have faced and overcome adversity. Read biographies, watch documentaries, or listen to podcasts featuring individuals who exemplify resilience. Their stories can motivate you and reinforce the belief that overcoming obstacles is possible.

Conclusion

Finding your inner strength when faced with obstacles is a transformative process that involves reflection, mindfulness, and an unwavering connection to your core purpose. By tapping into your inner resources and remaining focused on your "why," you empower yourself to navigate challenges with resilience and determination. Employing techniques for mental fortitude and endurance further fortifies your ability to confront obstacles head-on, fostering a mindset that thrives in the face of adversity. Remember, it is through overcoming challenges that we truly discover our strength and potential.

Chapter 11

Building Momentum

Momentum is an incredible force in both physics and life, serving as a catalyst for progress and success. In the context of personal growth and achievement, momentum plays a crucial role in harnessing the courage to begin and maintaining that momentum throughout our journeys. It acts as a powerful motivator that propels us forward, helping to overcome inertia and resistance that can often accompany new endeavours. Understanding how to cultivate and sustain this momentum can be transformative, allowing us to navigate the challenges of starting and pursuing our goals with greater ease and confidence.

The Nature of Momentum

At its core, momentum refers to the quantity of motion an object possesses. In life, this translates to the energy and drive we gain as we take action towards our goals. Much like a rolling snowball that gathers mass as it rolls down a hill, our actions create a build-up of momentum that can lead to significant progress. When we initiate an action—whether it's starting a new project, pursuing a fitness routine, or embarking on a career change—we generate energy that can propel us toward our desired outcomes.

The initial act of beginning is often the most challenging. It requires courage to step into the unknown, confront our fears, and embrace uncertainty. However, once we take that first step, we create a ripple effect that can generate momentum. This momentum is what carries us through the inevitable obstacles and setbacks that we encounter along the way. It creates a sense of progress that reinforces our commitment to our goals and fuels our motivation to continue moving forward.

The Connection Between Action and Momentum

One of the most critical aspects of momentum is the relationship between action and progress. Taking action is the first essential step in building momentum. When we take even the smallest action towards our goals, we ignite a chain reaction that can lead to larger accomplishments. Here's how this connection works:

1. **Creating Positive Feedback Loops**: Every action we take can lead to a sense of accomplishment, no matter how small. These feelings of achievement generate positive emotions that encourage us to keep going. If your goal is to write a book, setting a daily word count and achieving it—even if it's just a few sentences—provides a sense of progress. This achievement motivates you to write again the next day, creating a cycle of positive reinforcement.

2. **Building Confidence**: Each time we take action, we build our self-efficacy—the belief in our ability to succeed. This growing confidence is vital in overcoming the initial resistance to start. When we recognize that our efforts lead to progress, we become more willing to take additional steps, further amplifying our momentum. As we accumulate small victories, our belief in our capabilities solidifies, and we're more inclined to pursue more ambitious goals.

3. **Increasing Energy and Enthusiasm**: Taking action generates energy and enthusiasm, making it easier to stay engaged with our goals. As we see progress, we naturally feel more motivated to continue. The initial inertia we may have experienced dissipates, and we find ourselves in a

state of flow—fully immersed in our tasks and energized by the progress we're making.

Strategies to Build Momentum

To harness the power of momentum effectively, we must be intentional about how we initiate and maintain it. Here are some strategies to help you build and sustain momentum on your journey:

1. **Set Clear and Achievable Goals**: Begin by establishing specific, measurable, and achievable goals. Breaking down larger goals into smaller, manageable tasks allows you to experience quick wins along the way. Each time you complete a task, you create a sense of progress that fuels your momentum.

2. **Create a Routine**: Establishing a routine can help reinforce your commitment to your goals. Routines provide structure and predictability, making it easier to incorporate goal-oriented actions into your daily life. Consistency is key; when taking regular action becomes a habit, the momentum becomes self-sustaining.

3. **Embrace the Power of Start Small**: Don't be afraid to start small. The initial action can be as simple as dedicating ten minutes a day to your goal. The important thing is to take that first step, however minor it may seem. Starting small lowers

the barrier to entry and helps you build momentum gradually.

4. **Track Your Progress**: Keep a record of your accomplishments, no matter how small. Whether it's through a journal, a progress chart, or an app, tracking your progress allows you to visually see how far you've come. This tangible evidence of achievement reinforces your motivation and fuels your momentum.

5. **Celebrate Small Wins**: Acknowledge and celebrate your achievements, regardless of their size. Rewarding yourself for reaching milestones fosters a sense of accomplishment and encourages you to continue taking action. Celebrating small wins creates a positive emotional association with progress, reinforcing the desire to keep moving forward.

6. **Surround Yourself with Support**: Connect with others who share similar goals or aspirations. Engaging with a supportive community can provide encouragement and accountability, helping to sustain your momentum. Share your progress and celebrate achievements together, fostering a sense of camaraderie that propels you forward.

Conclusion

The role of momentum in the courage to begin cannot be overstated. It acts as a powerful driving force that propels us forward, helping to overcome inertia and resistance. By taking action, recognizing progress, and celebrating small wins, we can cultivate and sustain momentum throughout our journeys. As we embrace the courage to start, we unlock the potential for continuous growth, self-improvement, and lasting success.

Remember that every beginning is an opportunity to create momentum. Embrace the journey ahead with determination and enthusiasm, knowing that the momentum you build will carry you through challenges and propel you toward your dreams. As you take that first step, trust in the power of momentum to guide you, and never underestimate the transformative impact of the courage to begin.

Chapter 12

Celebrating Small Wins

In the journey of personal growth and achievement, it's easy to become fixated on the end goal, often overlooking the significant strides made along the way. However, recognizing and celebrating small wins is crucial for maintaining motivation and fostering a sense of accomplishment. Each step forward, no matter how small, contributes to the larger picture of success. By acknowledging these milestones, we not only boost our morale but also create a powerful momentum that propels us toward our bigger aspirations.

The Importance of Recognizing Progress

Celebrating small wins helps to reframe our perspective on progress. It allows us to shift our focus from what we haven't achieved to what we have accomplished. This positive reinforcement fosters a sense of fulfilment and encourages us to keep moving forward. Recognizing our progress serves several important purposes:

1. **Boosts Confidence**: Each small victory acts as a building block for confidence. When we take the time to acknowledge our achievements, we reinforce our belief in our abilities. This newfound confidence empowers us to tackle larger challenges with greater assurance.

2. **Enhances Motivation**: Celebrating small wins creates a sense of momentum. When we recognize our progress, we feel energized and motivated to continue pursuing our goals. This positive energy can be contagious, inspiring not just ourselves but also those around us.

3. **Reduces Feelings of Overwhelm**: Large goals can often feel daunting and unachievable. By breaking them down into smaller, manageable tasks and celebrating each completion, we make the journey less overwhelming. This approach helps to maintain focus and enthusiasm.

4. **Promotes Resilience**: In the face of setbacks and challenges, celebrating small wins provides a crucial reminder of our progress. It helps us maintain a positive outlook and strengthens our resilience, encouraging us to push through difficulties.

Acknowledging Even the Smallest Achievements

It is essential to cultivate the habit of recognizing and celebrating even the smallest achievements. This practice can take various forms, such as:

- **Keeping a Progress Journal**: Regularly jotting down your accomplishments, no matter how minor, can serve as a powerful reminder of your growth. This journal can be a source of inspiration during tough times, allowing you to reflect on how far you've come.

- **Setting Milestones**: Break your larger goals into smaller, achievable milestones, and celebrate when you reach each one. For example, if your goal is to write a book, celebrate completing a chapter, finishing a draft, or even just writing for a set number of days in a row.

- **Sharing Your Wins**: Do not hesitate to share your achievements with friends, family, or a support group. Sharing your successes fosters a sense of community and can lead to encouragement and additional motivation from others.

- **Rewarding Yourself**: Create a system of rewards for yourself. After achieving a small goal, treat yourself to something you enjoy, whether it's a favourite snack, a day off, or a small gift. This reward system reinforces the idea that your efforts are worthwhile.

Accelerating for Bigger Successes

Celebrating small wins isn't just about recognition; it's a strategic approach to building momentum for larger successes. Here's how acknowledging small achievements can lead to greater accomplishments:

1. **Establishing a Positive Feedback Loop**: Each time you celebrate a small win, you create a positive feedback loop. This encourages you to take on more significant challenges and reinforces your commitment to your goals.

2. **Building Consistency**: Recognizing progress helps you develop consistent habits. When you celebrate the completion of a task, you're more likely to repeat the behaviour, leading to a consistent effort toward your larger goals.

3. **Creating a Growth Mindset**: Acknowledging small wins fosters a growth mindset—an understanding that success is a journey filled with learning and development. This mindset

encourages you to embrace challenges and view setbacks as opportunities for growth.

4. **Sustaining progress During Setbacks**: When you encounter challenges, reflecting on your small wins can remind you of your capabilities and progress. This perspective can reignite your motivation and help you navigate through difficult times.

Conclusion

Celebrating small wins is a vital practice that nurtures motivation, confidence, and resilience. By recognizing and acknowledging even the smallest achievements, you create a positive environment that fosters momentum toward larger goals. Remember that success is a journey, and every step counts. Embrace the power of celebration, and allow it to propel you forward on your path to greatness. As you honour your progress, you'll find that each small win is not just an achievement but a building block for your future successes.

Chapter 13

Keep the End Goal in Mind

Keeping the end goal in mind is crucial for developing the courage to begin because it provides a sense of purpose and direction, helping us overcome initial hesitation and doubts. When we are clear about what we want to achieve, the path forward, even if challenging, becomes more meaningful, and the temporary discomforts of beginning something new feel worth enduring. The vision of a desirable outcome serves as a motivational anchor, reminding us why we are embarking on this journey in the first place.

Having a clear goal also helps us break down intimidating tasks into manageable steps, making the process of starting feel more approachable. By focusing on the ultimate destination, we are better able to push through fear, fatigue, or setbacks because we understand that these are just part of the journey toward something significant. This clarity of purpose fuels our resilience and keeps us committed, even when we encounter obstacles, knowing that each step forward is progress toward a greater vision.

In a practical sense, keeping the end goal in mind helps us navigate decisions and stay aligned with our core values. It ensures that our efforts are focused and meaningful, providing the courage to take that first step and the persistence to follow through. This mindset shift transforms beginnings from something daunting into opportunities for growth and fulfilment, empowering us to start with confidence and determination.

Always having the end goal in mind is a crucial element of building and maintaining momentum in any journey. It acts as your compass, guiding your actions and decisions while helping you stay focused on what truly matters. This mindset fosters resilience and determination, especially when faced with challenges or setbacks. Here are some strategies to help you effectively maintain your focus on the end goal:

Clarify Your Vision

- **Define What Success Looks Like**: Take the time to visualize your end goal in detail. What does success look like for you? Write down your vision, and be specific about the outcomes you desire.

- **Create a Vision Board**: A vision board is a visual representation of your goals and aspirations. Include images, quotes, and symbols that resonate with your end goal. Place it somewhere you can see it daily to remind you of your vision.

Establish Your "Why"

- **Identify Your Core Motivations**: Understanding why you want to achieve your goal is essential. What drives you? Is it personal fulfilment, financial stability, helping others, or something else? Your "why" will provide the motivation needed to persevere through challenges.

- **Write a Personal Mission Statement**: Craft a brief statement that encapsulates your values and aspirations related to your goal. This statement serves as a reminder of your purpose and can help you stay grounded when faced with distractions.

Set Intermediate Milestones

- **Break Down Your Goal**: Divide your end goal into smaller, achievable milestones. These intermediate steps serve as checkpoints on your journey, allowing you to measure progress and celebrate successes along the way.

- **Track Your Achievements**: Regularly assess your progress toward each milestone. Keeping track of your achievements reinforces your commitment and provides a sense of accomplishment, motivating you to keep moving forward.

Create a Roadmap

- **Develop an Action Plan**: Outline the specific steps needed to achieve your end goal. Having a clear roadmap helps you stay focused and organized, reducing feelings of overwhelm.

- **Stay Flexible**: While it's essential to have a plan, be open to adjusting it as needed. Life can be unpredictable, and being flexible allows you to navigate obstacles without losing sight of your ultimate goal.

Visualize the Journey

- **Imagine the Process**: Regularly visualize not just the end goal but also the journey toward it. Picture yourself taking each step and overcoming challenges along the way. This mental rehearsal helps build confidence and prepares you for the experiences ahead.

- **Focus on the Positive Outcomes**: Imagine how achieving your goal will impact your life. Envision the positive emotions and benefits that come with success, reinforcing your motivation to stay the course.

Stay Committed and Resilient

- **Reinforce Your Dedication**: Remind yourself of your commitment to your end goal regularly. Affirmations and self-talk can strengthen your resolve and keep you focused on what you want to achieve.

- **Develop Coping Strategies**: Anticipate challenges and setbacks, and prepare coping strategies to manage them effectively. Resilience is about bouncing back from difficulties while keeping your end goal in view.

Surround Yourself with Support

- **Build a Support Network**: Connect with individuals who share similar goals or values. Sharing your journey with others can provide encouragement, accountability, and inspiration.

- **Seek Mentorship**: If possible, find a mentor who has experience in your area of interest. Their guidance can help you stay focused and navigate the path toward your end goal.

Celebrate Progress

- **Acknowledge Milestones**: Celebrate your achievements, no matter how small. Recognizing your progress reinforces the importance of your end goal and keeps you motivated.

- **Reflect on Your Journey**: Take time to reflect on how far you've come and the lessons you've learned. This reflection reinforces your commitment and helps you stay connected to your ultimate vision.

Conclusion

Keeping the end goal in mind is essential for maintaining focus, motivation, and momentum in your journey. By clarifying your vision, understanding your "why," breaking down your goals, and celebrating your progress, you create a powerful framework that guides you toward success. Remember that the path to achieving your dreams may not always be linear, but with determination and clarity of purpose, you can navigate the challenges and continue moving forward. Embrace the journey, stay committed, and let your end goal inspire you to take consistent action each day.

Chapter 14

The Journey Continues

As we reach the conclusion of this exploration into the courage to begin, it becomes abundantly clear that starting is not merely a singular act but rather the initiation of a lifelong journey toward growth and self-improvement. Each time we muster the courage to take that first step—be it in pursuing a new goal, embarking on a project, or transitioning into a new phase of life—we open ourselves to a world of possibilities. This act of beginning is a powerful catalyst that propels us toward continuous development, shaping who we are and who we aspire to be.

The courage to begin is intertwined with the very essence of growth. Every new venture is an opportunity to learn, evolve, and challenge ourselves. It is in these moments of uncertainty and excitement that we discover our potential, uncover our strengths, and develop the resilience necessary to navigate life's complexities. Each start, whether met with triumph or setback, is a stepping stone on the path to self-discovery. It teaches us valuable lessons, enriches our experiences, and ultimately brings us closer to our true selves.

Never Stop Starting

One of the most empowering messages we can embrace is the idea of never stopping the process of starting. Life is a tapestry woven from countless beginnings—some grand and ambitious, others small and subtle. Each new goal or project we undertake adds colour and texture to our personal narrative. It's essential to recognize that every start, regardless of its magnitude, carries significance.

When you find yourself at a crossroads, unsure of which direction to take, remember that the act of starting itself is an achievement. Whether you're considering launching a new business, pursuing a hobby, or taking a leap into an unfamiliar career, summon the courage to take that first step. Embrace the uncertainty and allow it to fuel your determination. The journey ahead may be filled with challenges, but it's also brimming with opportunities for growth and transformation.

An Ongoing Journey

It's crucial to understand that beginnings are not isolated events; they are part of an ongoing journey of self-improvement. Each time we start anew, we cultivate a habit of resilience and adaptability. We learn to embrace change, to face our fears, and to celebrate our progress—no matter how small. This cyclical process of starting, learning, and growing reinforces the belief that we are capable of achieving our dreams, one step at a time.

As you navigate through life, keep the flame of curiosity alive. Seek new experiences, challenge yourself to step outside your comfort zone, and remain open to the lessons that each beginning brings. The courage to start again and again transforms not just your life but also the lives of those around you. Your willingness to embark on new adventures serves as an inspiration to others, encouraging them to pursue their aspirations.

Conclusion

In closing, the journey of life is a dynamic, ever-evolving adventure, where the courage to begin acts as a guiding compass. Embrace each new start with an open heart and a determined spirit. Acknowledge the growth that comes from every endeavour, whether it leads to success or lessons learned. As you continue to take those bold steps forward, remember that beginnings are not an endpoint; they are a vital part of the ongoing story of your life.

So, take a deep breath, trust in your ability to navigate the unknown, and never hesitate to begin anew. The world is full of opportunities waiting for you to explore, and every journey starts with the courage to take that first step. Your path to continuous growth and self-improvement is just a beginning away.

What Religious books guide us on The Courage to Begin

The concept of courage to begin is a common theme across many religious texts, reflecting a universal encouragement to overcome fear, uncertainty, and self-doubt to pursue one's purpose. These teachings offer guidance on finding strength within, trusting in a higher purpose, and taking the first step in faith, even when the path ahead is unclear.

The Bhagavad Gita

In the *Bhagavad Gita*, courage to begin is closely linked with duty and detachment from results. Krishna advises Arjuna to take action according to his *dharma* (duty) as a warrior, encouraging him to overcome doubt and fear. He reminds Arjuna that fear of failure should not hold him back, as courage arises from acting in alignment with one's values without attachment to the outcome. This teaches that true bravery lies in starting with purpose and faith, leaving the results to a higher power.

The Bible

In the *Bible*, courage to begin often comes through faith in God and His guidance. In the Book of Joshua, God instructs Joshua, "Be strong and courageous. Do not be afraid; do not be discouraged, for the Lord your God will be with you wherever you go" (Joshua 1:9). This call to courage emphasizes trust in divine presence and strength, encouraging followers to act with confidence, even when the path is challenging. Jesus also exemplifies this idea, teaching his disciples to overcome fear by putting their faith in God and beginning their journey of discipleship, regardless of trials.

The Quran

The *Quran* similarly encourages the faithful to begin with courage by trusting in Allah's wisdom and guidance. It emphasizes that fear and doubt should not prevent believers from taking righteous action, for Allah is with those who strive in His way. Surah Al-Imran (3:139) says, "So do not lose heart or be sad, for you will surely prevail if you are [true] believers." This assurance of divine support emphasizes that courage comes from faith, urging believers to start with purpose and resilience in Allah's name, confident in His support.

Buddhist Teachings

In Buddhism, the courage to begin is often about taking the first steps on the path to enlightenment by facing inner fears and illusions. The *Dhammapada*, a collection of the Buddha's teachings, emphasizes that courage comes from mindfulness and detachment from fear, stating, "With effort and heedfulness, discipline and self-mastery, let the wise make for themselves an island which no flood can overwhelm" (Dhammapada 25). Courage to begin, according to Buddhist philosophy, involves breaking free from attachments and taking action with awareness and compassion, even in the face of suffering.

Sikhism

In Sikhism, courage is tied to faith in God's will (Hukam) and the strength to start a righteous path. Guru Nanak and subsequent Gurus emphasize that courage to begin stems from trust in Waheguru (God) and an understanding that every action aligns with divine will. Guru Gobind Singh, the tenth Sikh Guru, taught Sikhs to have the courage to fight against injustice and uphold their beliefs despite adversity. This courage to begin is strengthened by trust in God's support, which empowers believers to pursue their path with both purpose and bravery.

www.ingramcontent.com/pod-product-compliance
Lightning Source LLC
LaVergne TN
LVHW010346200726
843507LV00010B/1666